UNDERSTAN~~~
ISLAM
BASIC PRINCIPLES

UNDERSTANDING
ISLAM
BASIC PRINCIPLES

Garnet
PUBLISHING

UNDERSTANDING ISLAM

Published by
Garnet Publishing Limited
8 Southern Court
South Street
Reading
RG1 4QS
UK

Copyright © Garnet Publishing

First Edition 2000

ISBN 1 85964 134 2

British Library Cataloguing-in-Publication Data
A catalogue record for this book is available from the British Library.

UNDERSTANDING ISLAM
BASIC PRINCIPLES

This book is based on the revision, editing and rearranging of three books. They are:

- *Basic Principles of Islam*
- *Understanding Islam and the Muslims*
- *The Status of Women in Islam.*

The objective of this book is to provide accessible and direct information about the basic principles of Islam as seen by Muslims themselves in order to facilitate the understanding of Islam by non-Muslims and non-Arabs. It is for this reason that the book answers frequently asked questions, including those on the status of women.

Contents

Mu'adh Ibn Jabal asked the Prophet Muhammad (may the blessings and peace of Allah be upon him): 'O Messenger of Allah, tell me of an act which will take me into Paradise and will keep me away from Hell-fire.' He said: 'You have asked me about a major matter, yet it is easy for him for whom Allah Almighty makes it easy. You should worship Allah, associating nothing with Him; you should perform the prayers; you should pay the *zakat*; you should fast in Ramadan; and you should make the pilgrimage to the House (*Al-Ka'bah*).' Then he said: 'Shall I not show you the gates of goodness? Fasting [which] is a shield; charity [which] extinguishes sin as water extinguishes fire; and the praying of a man in the depths of night.' Then he recited: ' "Who forsake their beds to cry unto their Lord in fear and hope, and spend of that which We have bestowed on them. No soul knoweth what is kept hid for it of joy, as a reward for what it used to do.' " Then he said: 'Shall I not tell you of the peak of the matter, its pillar, and its topmost part?' I said: 'Yes, O Messenger of Allah.' He said: 'The peak of the matter is Islam; the pillar is prayer; and its topmost part is *jihad*.' Then he said: 'Shall I not tell you of the controlling of all that?' I said: 'Yes, O Messenger of Allah,' and he took hold of his tongue and said: 'Restrain this.'

[This *Hadith* has been related and authenticated by *al-Tirmidhi*.]

سُورَةُ الْفَاتِحَةِ

بِسْمِ اللَّهِ الرَّحْمَٰنِ الرَّحِيمِ ﴿١﴾ الْحَمْدُ لِلَّهِ رَبِّ الْعَالَمِينَ ﴿٢﴾ الرَّحْمَٰنِ الرَّحِيمِ ﴿٣﴾ مَالِكِ يَوْمِ الدِّينِ ﴿٤﴾ إِيَّاكَ نَعْبُدُ وَإِيَّاكَ نَسْتَعِينُ ﴿٥﴾ اهْدِنَا الصِّرَاطَ الْمُسْتَقِيمَ ﴿٦﴾ صِرَاطَ الَّذِينَ أَنْعَمْتَ عَلَيْهِمْ غَيْرِ الْمَغْضُوبِ عَلَيْهِمْ وَلَا الضَّالِّينَ ﴿٧﴾

وَآتِيْنَاكَ سَبْعًا

1 - Surat Al-Fatiha

8

بسم الله الرحمن الرحيم

In the Name of Allah, Most Gracious, Most Merciful

PART I
GENERAL QUESTIONS

What is Islam?

Islam is not a new religion, but the same truth that God revealed through all His prophets to all people. For about one-fifth of the world's population, Islam is both a religion and a complete way of life. Muslims follow a religion of peace, mercy and forgiveness, and the majority have nothing to do with the extremely grave events that have been associated with their faith.

Who are the Muslims?

About one billion people from a vast range of races, nationalities and cultures across the globe – from the southern Philippines to Nigeria – are united by their common Islamic faith. About 18 per cent live in the Arab world; the world's largest Muslim community is in Indonesia; substantial parts of Asia and most of Africa are Muslim, while significant minorities are to be found in the former Soviet Union, China, North and South America, and Europe.

What do Muslims believe?

Muslims believe in One, Unique, Incomparable God; in the angels created by Him; in the prophets through whom His revelation was brought to mankind; in the Day of Judgement and individual accountability for actions; in God's complete authority over human destiny and in life after death. Muslims believe in a chain of prophets, starting with Adam and including Noah, Abraham, Ishmael, Isaac, Jacob, Joseph, Job, Moses, Aaron, David, Solomon, Elias, Jonah, John the Baptist and Jesus (Peace be upon them). But God's final message to man, a reconfirmation of the eternal message and a summing-up of all that went before, was revealed to Prophet Muhammad (Peace be upon him) through Angel Gabriel.

How does someone become a Muslim?

Someone becomes a Muslim simply by saying and believing: 'there is no god worthy of worship besides Allah, and Muhammad is the Messenger of Allah.' By this declaration the believer announces his or her faith in all of God's messengers and the scriptures revealed to them.

What does 'Islam' mean?

The Arabic word 'Islam' simply means 'submission', and derives from a word meaning 'peace'. In a religious context, it means complete submission to the will of 'Allah'. 'Allah' is the Arabic name for God, which is used

10

by both Arab Muslims and Arab Christians.

Why does Islam often seem strange?

Islam may seem exotic or even extreme in the modern world. Perhaps this is so because today religion does not dominate everyday life in the West, whereas Muslims always keep religion uppermost in their minds, and make no division between the secular and the sacred. They believe that the Divine Law, the *Shari'ah*, should be taken very seriously and this is why issues related to religion are still so important.

Do Islam and Christianity have different origins?

No. Together with Judaism, Christianity and Islam go back to Prophet and Patriarch Abraham, and their three prophets are directly descended from his sons – Muhammad from the eldest, Ishmael, and Moses and Mary, mother of Jesus (Peace upon them) from Isaac. Abraham established the settlement that today is the city of Mecca, and built the *Ka'bah* towards which all Muslims turn when they pray.

What is the *Ka'bah*?

The *Ka'bah* is the place of worship that God commanded Prophets Abraham and Ishmael to build over four thousand years ago. The building was constructed of stone. God commanded Abraham to summon all mankind to visit this place, and when pilgrims go there today they say: 'Here I am O Allah', in response to Abraham's summons.

2 - *Al Ka'bah*

12

Who is Muhammad?

Muhammad (Peace be upon him) was born in Mecca in the year 570, at a time when Christianity was not yet fully established in Europe. Since his father died before his birth, and his mother shortly afterwards, he was raised by his uncle from the respected tribe of *Quraysh*. As Muhammad grew up, he became known for his truthfulness, generosity and sincerity, so that he was sought after for his ability to arbitrate in disputes. The historians describe him as calm and contemplative.

Muhammad (Peace be upon him) was of a deep religious nature, and had long detested the decadence and idolatry of his society. It became his habit to meditate from time to time in the Cave of *Hira'* near the summit of Jabal al-Nur, the 'Mountain of Light', near Mecca.

How did Muhammad become a Prophet and Messenger of God?

At the age of forty, while engaged in a meditation retreat, Muhammad (Peace be upon him) received his first revelation from God through Angel Gabriel. This revelation, which continued for twenty-three years, is known as the *Qur'an*.

As soon as he began to recite the words he heard from Gabriel and to preach the truth that God had revealed to him, he and a small group of followers suffered bitter persecution, which grew so fierce that in the year 622 God commanded Muhammad to migrate along with his followers. This event, the *Hijrah* (migration), in which they left Mecca for the city of Yathrib some 260 miles to the north, marks the beginning of the Muslim calendar.

3 - *The site of Ghar Hira'*

After several years, the Prophet (Peace be upon him) and his followers were able to return to Mecca, where they forgave their enemies and established Islam. Before the Prophet (Peace be upon him) died in 632 at the age of sixty-three, the greater part of Arabia was Muslim, and within a century of his death Islam had spread as far as Spain in the West and as far as China in the East.

How did the spread of Islam affect the world?

Among the reasons for the rapid and peaceful spread of Islam was the simplicity of its doctrine: Islam calls for belief in only One God worthy of worship; it also repeatedly instructs man to use his powers of intelligence and observation.

Within a few years, great civilizations and schools were flourishing, for according to the Prophet (Peace be upon him), 'Seeking knowledge is an obligation for every Muslim.' The synthesis of Eastern and Western ideas and of new thought with the old brought about great advances in medicine, mathematics, physics, astronomy, geography, architecture, art, literature and history. Many crucial systems such as algebra, Arabic numerals and also the concept of the zero (vital to the advancement of mathematics), were transmitted to medieval Europe from Islam. Sophisticated instruments, which were to make possible the European voyages of discovery, were developed – including the astrolabe, the quadrant and good navigational maps.

What is the *Qur'an*?

The *Qur'an* is a record of the exact words revealed by God through Angel Gabriel to Prophet Muhammad (Peace be upon him). It was memorized by Muhammad (Peace be upon him) who then dictated God's words to his Companions. It was written down by scribes, who cross-checked it during Muhammad's lifetime. Not one word of its 114 chapters, *Suras*, has been changed over the centuries, so that the *Qur'an* is, in every detail, the unique and miraculous text that was revealed to Muhammad (Peace be upon him) fourteen centuries ago.

What is the *Qur'an* about?

The *Qur'an*, the last revealed Word of God, is the prime source of every Muslim's faith and practice. It deals with all the subjects that concern us as human beings: wisdom, doctrine, worship and law. However, its basic theme is the relationship between God and His creatures. At the same time, it provides guidelines for a just society, proper human conduct and an equitable economic system.

Are there any other sacred sources?

Yes, the *sunnah*, the sayings and deeds of the Prophet Muhammad (Peace be upon him), is the second authority for Muslims. A *Hadith* is a reliably transmitted report of what the Prophet Muhammad (Peace be upon him) said, did and approved or disapproved. Belief in the *sunnah* is a fundamental part of the Islamic faith.

Examples of the Prophet's sayings

The Prophet Muhammad (Peace be upon him) said:

'God has no mercy for the one who has no mercy for others.'

'None of you truly believes until he wishes for his brother what he wishes for himself.'

'He who eats his fill while his neighbour goes without food is not a true believer.'

'The truthful and trusty businessman is associated with the prophets, the saints and the martyrs.'

'The powerful is not he who knocks the other down; indeed the powerful is he who controls himself in a fit of anger.'

'God does not judge according to your bodies and appearances but He scans your hearts and looks into your deeds.'

'A man walking along a path felt very thirsty. Reaching a well he descended into it, drank his fill and came up. Then he saw a dog with its tongue hanging out, trying to lick up mud to quench its thirst. The man saw that the dog was feeling the same thirst as he had felt so he went down into the well again and filled his shoe with water and gave the dog a drink. God forgave his sins for this action. The Prophet (Peace be upon him) was asked: "Messenger of God, are we rewarded for kindness towards animals?" He replied: "There is a reward for kindness to every living thing." '

From the *Hadith* collections of Bukhari, Muslim, Tirmidhi and Bayhaqee.

PART II
PRINCIPLES OF THE ISLAMIC WAY OF LIFE

Nor can Goodness and Evil ﴿وَلَا تَسْتَوِى ٱلْحَسَنَةُ وَلَا ٱلسَّيِّئَةُ
Be equal. Repel (evil)
With what is better: ٱدْفَعْ بِٱلَّتِى هِىَ أَحْسَنُ فَإِذَا ٱلَّذِى
Then will he between whom
And yourself was hatred بَيْنَكَ وَبَيْنَهُ عَدَاوَةٌ كَأَنَّهُ وَلِيٌّ حَمِيمٌ
Become as it were
Your friend and intimate. ﴿٣٤﴾
Qur'an (41-34)

He has created the heavens ﴿خَلَقَ ٱلسَّمَوَتِ وَٱلْأَرْضَ
And the earth
In just proportions, بِٱلْحَقِّ وَصَوَّرَكُمْ فَأَحْسَنَ
And has given you shape,
And has made your shapes صُوَرَكُمْ وَإِلَيْهِ
Beautiful: and to Him
Is the final goal. ٱلْمَصِيرُ ﴿٣﴾﴾

Qur'an (64:3)

Glory to God Most High, full of Grace and Mercy; He created all, including man. To man He gave a special place in His Creation. He honoured man to be His regent and to that end endowed him with understanding, purified his affections, and gave him spiritual insight. Man should understand nature, understand himself and know God through His wondrous Signs, and glorify Him in truth, reverence, and unity.

For the fulfillment of this great trust man was given a Will, so that his acts should reflect God's universal Will and Law, and the free choice of his mind. Man should experience the sublime joy of being in harmony with the Infinite, and with the great drama of the world around him, and with his own spiritual growth.

Know that the life of this world	﴿أَعْلَمُوٓا۟ أَنَّمَا ٱلْحَيَوٰةُ ٱلدُّنْيَا
Is but play and amusement,	
Pomp and mutual boasting	لَعِبٌ وَلَهْوٌ وَزِينَةٌ وَتَفَاخُرٌۢ
And multiplying (in rivalry)	
Among yourselves, riches	بَيْنَكُمْ وَتَكَاثُرٌ فِى ٱلْأَمْوَٰلِ
And children.	
Here is a similitude	وَٱلْأَوْلَٰدِ كَمَثَلِ غَيْثٍ
How rain and the growth	
Which it brings forth, delights	أَعْجَبَ ٱلْكُفَّارَ نَبَاتُهُۥ ثُمَّ
(The hearts of) the farmers	
Soon it withers; you will	
See it grow yellow;	يَهِيجُ فَتَرَىٰهُ مُصْفَرًّا ثُمَّ
Then it becomes dry	
And crumbles away.	يَكُونُ حُطَٰمًا وَفِى ٱلْءَاخِرَةِ
But in the Hereafter	
Is a penalty severe	عَذَابٌ شَدِيدٌ وَمَغْفِرَةٌ مِّنَ

(For the devotees of wrong).
And forgiveness from God
And (His) Good Pleasure
(For the devotees of God).
And what is the life
Of this world,
But a matter of illusion.
Qur'an (57:20)

The average human being lives for about sixty years. Twenty years of this life is consumed by sleeping and approximately another ten in growing and learning. Taking into account another twenty years of working and worry, we are left with a meagre ten years in which to enjoy the 'realities' of life without the above 'prerequisites'. However, even with such freedom one still encounters physical pitfalls such as illness, anxiety and the natural process of aging. Overall, the life of this world may be summed up as a bitter-sweet game or test with no 'apparent' purpose.

Muslims believe that the limited life in this world merely serves as a transition towards the life eternal, Paradise. For those who strive in the right path there is a bounteous reward and for those who strive towards ignorance there is terrible punishment.

Muslims also believe that 'to be successful' in this world means to achieve one's aims and duties in this life and the life hereafter. Muslims invest in the worldly life through commitment to the family and invest in the hereafter through charity and almsgiving.

Muslims view the pleasures of this world as being petty and restrictive to our own senses and imagination, whereas the pleasures of the hereafter are boundless, as a gift from the Most Merciful, the Most Kind.

Islam means submission unto the will of God and those that submit unto the will of God are called Muslims.

Allah, an Arabic word that stands for the One and Only God, is Self-Subsisting; Eternal; neither Slumber nor Sleep overtaketh Him; the Source of Peace and Perfection, the Supreme; the Irresistible, no vision can comprehend Him but He comprehends all vision; who begets not and who is not begotten, and there is nothing like unto Him that can be imagined. Such is Allah, our Lord and your Lord; the only One deserving of worship and worthy of all Praise.

The Pillars of Faith in Islam

The Testimony of Faith reads: 'La Ilaha ila Allah, Muhammadun Rasul Allah' (There is no other object of worship but Allah and Muhammad is the Messenger of Allah).

Muslims also believe in the following.

- All the Prophets and Messengers of Allah, including Adam, Noah, Abraham, Moses, David, and Jesus.

- All the revealed Books of Allah, of which the Holy *Qur'an* is the last and most perfect one.

- All the Angels who are the spiritual beings of Allah.

- The Islamic doctrine that the power to act proceeds from Allah and every human being is morally responsible for his own actions.

- The Day of Resurrection and the Day of Judgement.

Islam is not a new religion. It is, in essence, the same message and guidance provided by God and revealed to all His prophets.

Say: We believe
In God, and in what
Has been revealed to us
And what was revealed
To Abraham, *Isma'il,*
Isaac, Jacob, and the Tribes,
And to (the Books)
Given to Moses, Jesus,
And the Prophets,
From their Lord:
We make no distinction
Between one and another
Among them, and to God do we
Bow our will (in Islam).
Qur'an (3:84)

﴿قُلْ ءَامَنَّا بِٱللَّهِ وَمَا أُنزِلَ
عَلَيْنَا وَمَا أُنزِلَ عَلَىٰ إِبْرَٰهِيمَ
وَإِسْمَٰعِيلَ وَإِسْحَٰقَ
وَيَعْقُوبَ وَٱلْأَسْبَاطِ وَمَا
أُوتِيَ مُوسَىٰ وَعِيسَىٰ وَٱلنَّبِيُّونَ
مِن رَّبِّهِمْ لَا نُفَرِّقُ بَيْنَ أَحَدٍ
مِّنْهُمْ وَنَحْنُ لَهُ
مُسْلِمُونَ ﴾ ۝

The message that was revealed to the Prophet Muhammad (Peace be upon him) is Islam in its comprehensive, complete and final form.

Let there be no compulsion
In religion: Truth stands out
Clear from error: whoever
Rejects evil and believes
In Allah (One God) has grasped

﴿لَا إِكْرَاهَ فِي ٱلدِّينِ قَد
تَّبَيَّنَ ٱلرُّشْدُ مِنَ ٱلْغَيِّ فَمَن

The most trustworthy
Hand-hold, that never breaks.
And Allah hears
And knows all things.
Qur'an (2:256)

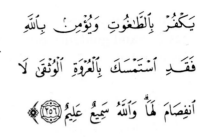

No Chosen People

Islam rejects the idea of a chosen people, making faith in the one God and good action the sole key to Paradise. However, the *Qur'an* praises the nation *(ummah)* of Islam for its praiseworthy qualities.
Qur'an (3:40).

The 'Five Pillars' of Islam?

The Five Pillars of Islam are Testimony, Prayer, Zakat, Fasting and Pilgrimage. We will look at each of these in turn.

Testimony

'There is no god except Allah and Muhammad is His Messenger'.
This declaration of faith is called the *Shahadah,* a simple formula that all the faithful pronounce. In Arabic, the first part is 'La Ilaha ila Allah' (there is no god except Allah); The second part of the *Shahadah* is 'Muhammadun Rasul Allah' (Muhammad is the Messenger of Allah).

Prayer

Salat is the name for the obligatory prayers that are performed five times a day; they are a direct link between the worshipper and God. There is no hierarchical authority in Islam and no priests, so the prayers are led by a learned person who knows the *Qur'an*, chosen by the congregation. These five prayers contain verses from the *Qur'an* and are said in Arabic, the language of the Revelation, but personal supplication can be offered in one's own language.

Prayers are performed at dawn, noon, mid-afternoon, sunset and nightfall, and thus determine the rhythm of the entire day. Although it is preferable to worship together in a mosque, Muslims may pray almost anywhere, such as in fields, offices, factories and universities. Visitors to the Muslim world are struck by the centrality of prayers in daily life. Below is a translation of the Call to Prayer.

Allah is most great, Allah is most great.
Allah is most great, Allah is most great.
I testify that there is no god except Allah.
I testify that there is no god except Allah.
I testify that Muhammad is the Messenger of Allah.
I testify that Muhammad is the Messenger of Allah.
Come to prayer! Come to prayer!
Come to success (in the life and the Hereafter)!
Come to success!
Allah is most great, Allah is most great.
There is no god except Allah.

Zakat

One of the most important principles of Islam is that all things belong to God, and that wealth is therefore held by human beings in trust. The word *zakat* means both 'purification' and 'growth'. Our possessions are purified by setting aside a portion for those in need and, like the pruning of plants, this cutting back balances and encourages new growth.

Each Muslim calculates his or her own *zakat* individually. For most purposes, this involves the payment each year of 2.5 per cent of one's surplus savings. A pious person may also give as much as he or she pleases as *sadaqah*, and does so preferably in secret. Although this word can be translated as voluntary charity, it has a wider meaning. The Prophet (Peace be upon him) said: 'Even meeting your brother with a cheerful face is charity.'

The Prophet (Peace be upon him) said: 'Charity is a necessity for every Muslim.' He was asked: 'What if a person has nothing?' The Prophet (Peace be upon him) replied: 'He should work with his own hands for his benefit and then give something out of such earnings in charity.' The Companions asked: 'What if he is not able to work?' The Prophet (Peace be upon him) said: 'He should help the poor and the needy persons.' The Companions further asked: 'What if he cannot do even that?' The Prophet (Peace be upon him) said: 'He should urge others to do good.' The Campanions said: 'What if he lacks that also?' The Prophet (Peace be upon him) said: 'He should check himself from doing evil. That is also charity.'

Fasting

Every year in the month of Ramadan, all Muslims fast from first light until sundown, abstaining from food, drink and sexual relations. Those who are sick, elderly or on a journey, and women who are pregnant or nursing, are permitted to break the fast and make up an equal number of days later in the year. If they are physically unable to do this, they must feed a needy person for every day missed. Children begin to fast (and to observe the prayer) from puberty, although many start earlier.

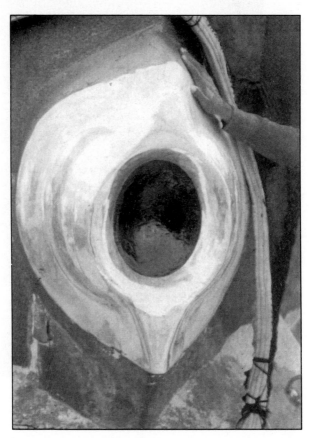

4 - The Black
   Stone

Although the fast is considered beneficial to health, it is regarded principally as a method of self-purification. By cutting oneself off from worldly comforts, even for a short time, a fasting person gains true sympathy with those who go hungry, which leads to growth in one's spiritual life.

5 - The door of the Holy *Ka'bah*

Pilgrimage

The annual pilgrimage to Mecca - the *Hajj* – is an obligation only for those who are physically and financially able to perform it. Nevertheless, about two million people go to Mecca each year from every corner of the globe providing a unique opportunity for those of different nations to meet one another.

Although Mecca is always filled with visitors, the annual *Hajj* begins in the twelfth month of the Islamic year (which is lunar, not solar, so that *Hajj* and Ramadan fall sometimes in summer, sometimes in winter). Pilgrims wear special clothes – simple garments that strip away distinctions of class and culture, so that all stand equal before God.

The Holy *Qur'an*

The *Qur'an*, which is in the Arabic language, is the complete book of guidance for mankind. It is the sacred book of the Muslims and the main source of law in Islam. The whole of the *Qur'an* is from Allah. Each word of it is a revealed word. It was sent down to Muhammad (Peace be upon him) through the Angel Gabriel, was revealed piecemeal and completed over a period of twenty-three years.

No other book in the world can match the *Qur'an*, even with respect to its recording and preservation. The astonishing fact about this book of Allah is that it has remained unchanged, even to the dot, over the last fourteen hundred years. The *Qur'an* was recorded as soon as it was revealed under the personal supervision of

Prophet Muhammad (Peace be upon him), and exists today in its original form, unaltered and undistorted. It is a living miracle in the sense that it has survived so many centuries without suffering any change.

The *Qur'anic* message goes beyond time and space. Every word of it, even the smallest signs, are intact in the hearts of thousands of Muslims who continue to memorize and recite it every day. No variation of text can be found. You can check this for yourself by listening to the recitation of Muslims from different parts of the world.

Allah, the Almighty, has Himself taken the responsibility of preserving the *Qur'an* and says: 'Surely, we have revealed this reminder and lo, we verily are its guardian. (15:9).

The *Qu'ran* is a living proof of the existence of Allah, the All-Powerful. It is also a testimony of the validity of the Islamic way of life for all times. Unlike the languages of other revealed books, the language of the *Qur'an*, Arabic, is a living, dynamic and very rich language. Millions of people all over the world speak and use Arabic in their daily lives. This is a further testimony to the unchanging character of the *Qur'an*.

The subject matter of the *Qur'an* is man and his ultimate goal in life.

Qur'anic teachings cover all areas of this life and the life after death. It contains principles, doctrines and directions for every sphere of human activity. The theme of the *Qur'an* consists broadly of three fundamental beliefs: *Tawhid, Risalah* (the Message as given to the Prophet) and *Akhirah* (The Afterlife). *Tawhid* (that is, the doctrine of the Oneness of God) is the basic theme of the *Qur'an*. All the prophets and messengers of Allah called people towards *Tawhid*. The Qur'an gives a picturesque description of the Paradise that will be awarded to the true obedient servants of Allah. The severe punishment to be meted out to the evil-doers has also been depicted vividly in the Qur'an.

The *Qur'an* urges people to follow its guidance and teachings. The success of human beings on this earth and in life after death depends on obedience to the *Qur'anic* teachings. We cannot perform our duties as the servants of Allah and His agents if we do not follow the *Qur'an*. The *Qur'an* urges us to work for the supremacy of Islam and for the removal of all evils.

The superb style of the *Qur'an* has a tremendous effect on its readers. It totally changes the pattern of life of those who believe and practice its teachings. It leaves a soothing effect on the mind of the reader, even if he does not fully understand its meaning.

The Life of the Prophet

The Prophet Muhammad (Peace be upon him) rose from being an orphan (having lost his father before his birth and his mother while a child of only five) to be the greatest force known to history for the moral, spiritual and social regeneration of a fallen humanity. While still a young man he was known and respected for his purity and integrity. His nickname then was al-Amin, which means trustworthy and righteous *par excellence*. For thirteen years, he and his small group of followers were subjected to the worst persecutions, ostracism, torture and social boycott. Ultimately, he had to flee Mecca along with his followers, seeking refuge in Yathrib – 250 miles away from Mecca. His opponents, however, did not leave him alone there. They stirred up the tribes against him and made attack after attack upon him in the distant refuge, in order to put an end to what they considered to be a menace to their inherited superstitions and iniquitous hegemony. In the encounters that followed, the superior morale of the Muslims born of faith in a noble cause triumphed over all the forces ranged against them.

Unlike common victors in history who visit all sorts of punishment on the vanquished, the Prophet (Peace be upon him), in the highest spirit of chivalry, which Islam teaches towards a fallen foe, not only gave his blood-thirsty enemies a general amnesty, but also extended towards them a hand of fellowship. Thereby, he welded the whole populace into a solid brotherhood, inaugurating the new era where morals and social justice reigned supreme.

From an orphan to head of state, the Prophet Muhammad (Peace be upon him) saw life in all its vicissitudes, and went through its manifold ups and downs. To all these situations he brought a lustre of his own, thereby blazing in this dark and dismal struggle of life the path of truth, honour and dignity to seekers after truth in all walks of life. Above all, the sense that he was a humble servant of God, which was the sum and substance of his mission, never left him.

Even as the ruler of the vast domains of the Arabian peninsula, Prophet Muhammad (Peace be upon him) lived the life of a plain common man, washing and stitching his own clothes, milking his goats, mending his shoes and lending a helping hand in the household work.

In Prophet Muhammad (Peace be upon him) were fulfilled the prophecies of both Moses (Peace be upon him) and Jesus (Peace be upon him) as to the advent of a prophet who would bring a new law and lead the people unto all truth.

The Lord thy God will raise unto thee a Prophet (Peace be upon him) from the midst of thee, of thy brethren, like unto me; unto him ye shall hearken.

Deuteronomy (18:15)

I have yet many things to say unto you, but ye cannot bear them now. How be it when he, the spirit of truth, to come, he will guide you into all truth; for he shall not speak of himself, but whatsoever he shall hear, that shall he speak, and he will show you things to come.

John (16:12 – 13)

The Family

The family is the foundation of Islamic society. The peace and security offered by a stable family unit is greatly valued and seen as essential for the spiritual growth of its members. A harmonious social order is created by the existence of extended families; and children are treasured and rarely leave home until the time they marry.

Family, society and ultimately the whole of mankind is treated by Islam on an ethical basis. Differentiation in sex is neither a credit nor a drawback for the sexes. Therefore, when we talk about the status of women in Islam, it should not lead us to think that Islam has no specific guidelines, limitations, responsibilities and obligations for men. What makes one valuable and respectable in the eyes of Allah, the Creator of mankind and the universe, is neither one's prosperity, position, intelligence, physical strength nor beauty, but only one's consciousness and awareness of Allah. However, since in Western culture and in cultures influenced by the West, there exists a disparity between men and women, there is more need for stating Islam's position on these important issues in a clear way.

The status of women in society is neither a new issue nor is it a fully settled one. The position of Islam on this issue has been among the subjects presented to the Western reader with the least objectivity.

This section is intended to provide a brief and authentic exposition of what Islam stands for in this regard. The teachings of Islam are based essentially on the *Qur'an* (God's revelation) and *Hadith* (sayings of Prophet Muhammad).

The *Qur'an* and the *Hadith*, properly and unbiasedly understood, provide the basic sources of authentication for any position or view that is attributed to Islam.

We start with a brief survey of the status of women in the pre-Islamic era, then focus on the following major questions.

● What is the position of Islam regarding the status of woman in society?

● How similar or different is that position from 'the spirit of the time', which was dominant when Islam was revealed?

● How would this compare with the 'rights' that were finally gained by women in recent decades?

Historical Perspectives on Women

One major objective of this chapter is to provide a fair evaluation of what Islam contributed (or failed to contribute) towards the restoration of women's dignity and rights. In order to achieve this objective, it may be useful to review briefly how women were treated in general in previous civilizations and religions, especially those that preceded Islam (Pre-10 CE)[1] Part of the information provided here, however, describes the status of women as late as the nineteenth century, more than twelve centuries after Islam.

Women in Ancient Civilization

Describing the status of the Indian woman, *Encyclopedia Britannica* states:

In India, subjection was a cardinal principle. Day and night must women be held by their protectors in a state of dependence says Manu. The rule of inheritance was agnatic, that is descent traced through males to the exclusion of females.[2]

In Hindu scriptures, the description of a good wife is as follows:

A woman whose mind, speech and body are kept in subjection, acquires high renown in this world and, in the next, the same abode with her husband.[3]

---

1 CE stands for Christian Era.
2 *Encyclopedia Britannica,* 11th ed., 1911, vol. 28, p. 782.
3 In Mace, David and Vera, *Marriage East and West*, Dolphin Books, Doubleday and Co., Inc., N.Y., 1960.

In Athens, women were no better off than either the Indian or Roman women.

Athenian women were always minors, subject to some male – to their father, to their brother, or to some of their male kin.[4]

Her consent in marriage was not generally thought to be necessary and:

She was obliged to submit to the wishes of her parents, and receive from them her husband and her lord, even though he was a stranger to her.[5]

A Roman wife was described by an historian as:

A babe, a minor, a ward, a person incapable of doing or acting anything according to her own individual taste, a person continually under the tutelage and guardianship of her husband.[6]

In *Encyclopedia Britannica*, we find a summary of the legal status of women in the Roman civilization.[7]

In Roman Law a woman was even in historic times completely dependent. If married she and her property passed into the power of her husband . . . the wife was the purchased property of her husband and, like a slave, acquired only for his benefit. A woman could not exercise any civil or public office . . . could not be a witness, surety, tutor or curator; she could not adopt or be adopted, or make will or contract.

Among the Scandinavian races women were:

---

4 Allen, E.A., *History of Civilization*, vol. 3, p. 444.
5 Ibid., p. 443.
6 Ibid., p. 550.
7 *Encyclopedia Britannica*, 11th ed., 1911, op. cit., vol. 28, p. 782.

. . . under perpetual tutelage, whether married or unmarried. As late as the Code of Christian V, at the end of the seventeenth century, it was enacted that if a woman married without the consent of her tutor he might have, if he wished, her goods during her life.[8]

According to the English Common Law:

. . . all real property that a wife held at the time of a marriage became a possession of her husband. He was entitled to the rent from the land and to any profit that might be made from operating the estate during the joint life of the spouses. As time passed, the English courts devised means to forbid a husband's transferring real property without the consent of his wife, but he still retained the right to manage it and to receive the money that it produced. As to a wife's personal property, the husband's power was complete. He had the right to spend it as he saw fit.[9]

Only by the late nineteenth century did the situation start to improve.

By a series of acts starting with the Married women's Property Act in 1870, amended in 1882 and 1887, married women achieved the right to own property and to enter contracts on a par with spinsters, widows and divorcees.[10]

As late as the nineteenth century an authority in ancient law, Sir Henry Maine, wrote:

No society which preserves any tincture of Christian

---

8 Ibid., p. 783.
9 *Encyclopedia Americana* (International edition), vol. 29, p. 108.
10 *Encyclopedia Britannica,* 1968, vol. 23, p. 624.

institutions is likely to restore to married women the personal liberty conferred on them by the Middle Roman Law.[11]

In his essay '*The subjection of women*', John Stuart Mill wrote:

We are continually told that civilization and Christianity have restored to the woman her just rights. Meanwhile the wife is the actual bondservant of her husband; no less so, as far as the legal obligation goes, than slaves commonly so called.[12]

Before moving on to the *Qur'anic* decrees concerning the status of women, a few Biblical decrees may shed more light on the subject, thus providing a better basis for an impartial evaluation. In Mosaic Law, the wife was betrothed. Explaining this concept, *Encyclopedia Biblica* states:

To betroth a wife to oneself meant simply to acquire possession of her by payment of the purchase money; the betrothed is a girl for whom the purchase money has been paid.[13]

From the legal point of view, the consent of the girl was not necessary for the validation of her marriage.

The girl's consent is unnecessary and the need for it is nowhere suggested in the Law.[14]

As to the right of divorce, we read in the *Encyclopedia Biblica*:

The woman being man's property, his right to divorce her

---

11 Quoted in Mace, *Marriage East and West*, op. cit., p. 81.
12 Ibid., pp. 82 – 83.
13 *Encyclopedia Biblica*, 1902, vol. 3, p. 2942.
14 Ibid., p. 2942.

follows as a matter of course.[15]

The right to divorce was held only by man.

In the Mosaic Law divorce was a privilege of the husband only . . .[16]

The position of the Christian church until recent centuries seems to have been influenced by both Mosaic Law and by the streams of thought that were dominant in its contemporary culture. In their book, *Marriage East and West*, David and Vera Mace[17] wrote:

Let no one suppose, either, that our Christian heritage is free of such slighting judgements. It would be hard to find anywhere a collection of more degrading references to the female sex than the early Church Fathers provide. Lecky, the famous historian, speaks of these fierce incentives which form so conspicuous and so grotesque a portion of the writing of the Fathers) . . . woman was represented as the door of hell, as the mother of all human ills. She should be ashamed at the very thought that she is a woman. She should live in continual penance on account of the curses she has brought upon the world. She should be ashamed of her dress, for it is the memorial of her fall. She should be especially ashamed of her beauty, for it is the most potent instrument of the devil. One of the most scathing of these attacks on woman is that of Tertullian: do you know that you are each an Eve? The

---

15 Ibid., p. 2947.
16 *Encyclopedia Britannica*, 11th ed., op. cit., p. 782.
   It should be noted here that such interpretations by religious institutions do not necessarily conform to what the Muslim believes to be the original version of all revealed religions, which is believed to be essentially the same throughout history.
17 Mace, *Marriage East and West*, op. cit., pp. 80 – 81.

sentence of God on this sex of yours lives in this age: the guilt must of necessity live too. You are the devil's gateway: you are the unsealer of that forbidden tree; you are the first deserters of the divine law; you are she who persuades him whom the devil was not valiant enough to attack. You destroyed so easily God's image, man. On account of your desert that is death – even the Son of God had to die.

Not only did the Church affirm the inferior status of women but also it deprived her of legal rights she had previously enjoyed.

Women in Islam

In the midst of the darkness that engulfed the world, the divine revelation echoed in the wide desert of Arabia with a fresh, noble and universal message to humanity:

O Mankind, keep your duty to your Lord who created you from a single soul and from it created its mate (of same kind) and from them twain has spread a multitude of men and women.[18]

Qur'an (4:1).

A scholar who pondered about verse 4:1 states:

It is believed that there is no text, old or new, that deals with the humanity of the woman from all aspects with such amazing brevity, eloquence, depth and originality as this divine decree.[19]

---

18 'From it' here refers to the kind – that is, 'from the same kind, or of like nature, God created its mate'. There is no trace in the *Qur'an* to a parallel of the Biblical concept that Eve was created from one of Adam's ribs. See Yusuf Ali, *The Holy Qur'an*, note no. 504.

19 El-Khouly, Al-Bahiy, *'Min Usus Kadiyat Al-Mar'ah' Al-Waa'y Al-Islami*, Ministry of *Wakf*, Kuwait, vol. 3, no. 27, june 9, 1967, p. 17.

Stressing this noble and natural conception, the *Qur'an* states the following.

﴿ ۞ هُوَ ٱلَّذِى خَلَقَكُم مِّن نَّفْسٍ وَٰحِدَةٍ وَجَعَلَ مِنْهَا زَوْجَهَا لِيَسْكُنَ إِلَيْهَا ﴾

He [God] it is who did create you from a single soul and therefrom did create his mate, that he might dwell with her (in love) ...
Qur'an (7:189)

﴿فَاطِرُ ٱلسَّمَٰوَٰتِ وَٱلْأَرْضِ جَعَلَ لَكُم مِّنْ أَنفُسِكُمْ أَزْوَٰجًا﴾

The *Qur'an* also states:
... the Creator of heavens and earth: He has made for you pairs from among yourselves ...
Qur'an (42:11)

﴿وَٱللَّهُ جَعَلَ لَكُم مِّنْ أَنفُسِكُمْ أَزْوَٰجًا وَجَعَلَ لَكُم مِّنْ أَزْوَٰجِكُم بَنِينَ وَحَفَدَةً وَرَزَقَكُم مِّنَ ٱلطَّيِّبَٰتِ أَفَبِٱلْبَٰطِلِ يُؤْمِنُونَ وَبِنِعْمَتِ ٱللَّهِ هُمْ يَكْفُرُونَ ۞﴾

41

Finally, the *Qur'an* says:

And Allah has given you mates of your own nature, and has given you from your mates children and grandchildren, and has made provision of good things for you. Is it then in vanity that they believe and in the grace of God that they disbelieve?
Qur'an (16:72)

The remainder of this chapter outlines the position of Islam regarding the status of woman in society from its various aspects – spiritually, socially, economically and politically.

The spiritual aspect

The *Qur'an* provides clear-cut evidence that women are completely equated with men in the sight of God in terms of their rights and responsibilities. The *Qur'an* states:

$$ \text{﴿ كُلُّ نَفْسٍ بِمَا كَسَبَتْ رَهِينَةٌ ﴿٣٨﴾ ﴾} $$

Every soul will be [held] in pledge for its deeds.
Qur'an (74:38)

It also states:

$$ \text{﴿ فَاسْتَجَابَ لَهُمْ رَبُّهُمْ أَنِّي لَا أُضِيعُ عَمَلَ عَامِلٍ مِّنكُم مِّن ذَكَرٍ أَوْ أُنثَىٰ بَعْضُكُم مِّنْ بَعْضٍ ﴾} $$

... So their Lord accepted their prayers [saying]: 'I will not

suffer to be lost the work of any of you whether male or female. You proceed one from another . . .'
Qur'an (3:195)

بِسْمِ اللَّهِ ﴿مَنْ عَمِلَ صَالِحًا مِّن ذَكَرٍ أَوْ أُنثَىٰ وَهُوَ مُؤْمِنٌ فَلَنُحْيِيَنَّهُ حَيَوٰةً طَيِّبَةً وَلَنَجْزِيَنَّهُمْ أَجْرَهُم بِأَحْسَنِ مَا كَانُوا يَعْمَلُونَ ﴿٩٧﴾﴾

Other verses from the *Qur'an* related to this subject include those that follow.

Whoever works righteousness, man or woman, and has faith, verily to him will We give a new life that is good and pure, and We will bestow on such their reward according to their actions.
Qur'an (16:97); see also 4:124

According to the *Qur'an*, a woman is not blamed for Adam's first mistake. Both were jointly wrong in their disobedience to God, both repented and both were forgiven (*Qur'an* 2:36, 7:20 – 24). In fact, in verse 20:121, Adam was specifically blamed.

In terms of religious obligations, such as the Daily Prayers, Fasting, Almsgiving and Pilgrimage, women are no different from men. Indeed, in some cases women have certain advantages over men – for example, they are exempted from daily prayers, from fasting during their menstrual periods and for forty days after childbirth. A woman is also exempted from fasting during pregnancy and when nursing her baby if there is any threat to her health or that of her baby. If the missed fasting is obligatory (during the month of Ramadan), a woman can make up for the missed days whenever she can. She does not have to make up for the prayers missed for any of the above reasons. Although women can (and did) go into the mosque during the days of the Prophet and thereafter attended the Friday congregational prayers, this is optional for them but it is mandatory for men (on Fridays).

This is clearly a tender touch of the Islamic teachings, for they are considerate of the fact that a woman may be nursing or caring for her baby, and thus may be unable to go out to the mosque at the time of the prayers. They also take into account the physiological and psychological changes associated with her natural female functions.

The social aspect

The social aspect of women in Islam can be separated into three different parts of their lives: when they are children and adolescents, when they become wives and when they become mothers.

As a child and an adolescent

Despite the social acceptance of female infanticide among some Arabian tribes, the *Qur'an* forbade this custom, and considered it a crime like any other murder.

And when the female (infant) buried alive is questioned, for
what crime she was killed.
Qur'an (81:8–9).

﴾ وَإِذَا ٱلْمَوْءُۥدَةُ سُبِلَتْ ۝ بِأَىِّ ذَنۢبٍ قُتِلَتْ ۝ ﴿

Criticizing the attitudes of such parents who reject their
female children, the Qur'an states:

﴾ وَإِذَا بُشِّرَ أَحَدُهُم بِٱلْأُنثَىٰ ظَلَّ وَجْهُهُۥ مُسْوَدًّا وَهُوَ كَظِيمٌ ۝

يَتَوَٰرَىٰ مِنَ ٱلْقَوْمِ مِن سُوٓءِ مَا بُشِّرَ بِهِۦٓ أَيُمْسِكُهُۥ عَلَىٰ هُونٍ أَمْ يَدُسُّهُۥ فِى

ٱلتُّرَابِ أَلَا سَآءَ مَا يَحْكُمُونَ ۝ ﴿

When news is brought to one of them, of [the birth] of a
female [child], his face darkens and he is filled with inward
grief! With shame does he hide himself from his people
because of the bad news he has had! Shall he retain her on
[sufferance] and contempt, or bury her in the dust? Ah! What
an evil [choice] they decide on?

Qur'an (16:58–59)

Far from saving the girl's life so that she may later suffer
injustice and inequality, Islam requires kind and just
treatment of her. Among the sayings of Prophet

Muhammad (Peace be upon him) in this regard are the following.

Whosoever has a daughter and he does not bury her alive, does not insult her, and does not favour his son over her, God will enter him into Paradise.

Ibn Hanbal (No. 1957)

Whosoever supports two daughters till they mature, he and I will come on the Day of Judgement as this (and he pointed with his two fingers held together). A similar *Hadith* deals in like manner with one who supports two sisters.

Ibn Hanbal (No. 2104)

The right of females to seek knowledge is not different from that of males. Prophet Muhammad (Peace be upon him) said:

Seeking knowledge is mandatory for every Muslim.

Al-Bayhaqi

Muslim as used here includes both males and females.[20]

As a wife

The *Qur'an* clearly indicates that marriage is sharing between the two halves of society, and that its objectives, perpetuating human life, are emotional well-being and spiritual harmony. Its bases are love and mercy. Among

---

20 Some less authentic versions add 'male and female.' The meaning, however, is sound etomologically even as it is consistent with the overall nature of Islamic duties in applying equally to males and females unless special exemptions are specified.

the most impressive verses in the *Qur'an* about marriage is the following.

$$\text{﴿وَمِنْ ءَايَـٰتِهِۦٓ أَنْ خَلَقَ لَكُم مِّنْ أَنفُسِكُمْ أَزْوَٰجًا لِّتَسْكُنُوٓا إِلَيْهَا وَجَعَلَ بَيْنَكُم مَّوَدَّةً وَرَحْمَةً إِنَّ فِى ذَٰلِكَ لَءَايَـٰتٍ لِّقَوْمٍ يَتَفَكَّرُونَ ۝﴾}$$

And among His signs is this: That He created mates for you from yourselves that you may find rest, peace of mind in them, and He ordained between you love and mercy. Lo, herein indeed are signs for people who reflect.
Qur'an (30:21)

According to Islamic Law, women cannot be forced to marry anyone without their consent.

Ibn Abbas reported that a girl came to the Messenger of God, Muhammad (Peace be upon him) and reported that her father had forced her to marry without her consent. The Messenger of God gave her the choice ... (between accepting the marriage or invalidating it).
Ibn Hanbal (No. 2469)

In another version, the girl said:

Actually I accept this marriage but I wanted to let women know that parents have no right (to force a husband on them).
Ibn-Maja (No. 1873)

Besides all other provisions for her protection at the time of marriage, it was specifically decreed that a woman has

47

the full right to her *Mahr*, a marriage gift, which is presented to her by her husband and is included in the nuptial contract, and that such ownership does not transfer to her father or husband. The concept of *Mahr* in Islam is neither an actual or symbolic price for the woman, as was the case in certain cultures, but rather it is a gift symbolizing love and affection.

The *rules for married life* in Islam are clear and in harmony with upright human nature. In consideration of the physiological and psychological make-up of man and woman, both have equal rights and claims on one another, except for one responsibility – that of leadership. This is a matter that is natural in any collective life and which is consistent with the nature of man. The Qur'an thus states:

$$\text{﴿وَلَهُنَّ مِثْلُ ٱلَّذِى عَلَيْهِنَّ بِٱلْمَعْرُوفِ وَلِلرِّجَالِ عَلَيْهِنَّ دَرَجَةٌ﴾}$$

And they [women] have rights similar to those [of men] over them, and men are a degree above them.

Qur'an (2:228)

Such degree is *Qiwama* (maintenance and protection). This refers to that natural difference between the sexes that entitles the weaker sex to protection. It implies no superiority or advantage before the law. Yet man's role of leadership in relation to his family does not mean the husband's dictatorship over his wife. Islam emphasizes the importance of taking counsel and mutual agreement in family decisions. The *Qur'an* gives us an example.

$$\text{﴿فَإِنْ أَرَادَا فِصَالًا عَن تَرَاضٍ مِّنْهُمَا وَتَشَاوُرٍ فَلَا جُنَاحَ عَلَيْهِمَا﴾}$$

48

... If they [husband and wife] desire to wean the child by mutual consent and [after] consultation, there is no blame on ...

Qur'an (2:233)

Over and above her basic rights as a wife comes the right that is emphasized by the *Qur'an* and is strongly recommended by the Prophet (Peace be upon him): kind treatment and companionship. The Qur'an states:

$$\text{﴿وَإِن كَرِهْتُمُوهُنَّ فَعَسَىٰ أَن تَكْرَهُواْ شَيْئًا وَيَجْعَلَ ٱللَّهُ فِيهِ خَيْرًا كَثِيرًا ۝﴾}$$

... But consort with them in kindness, for if you hate them it may happen that you hate a thing wherein God has placed much good.

Qur'an (4:19)

Prophet Muhammad (Peace be upon him) said:

The best of you is the best to his family and I am the best among you to my family.

The most perfect believers are the best in conduct and the best of you are those who are best to their wives.

Behold, many women came to Muhammad's wives complaining against their husbands [because they beat them] – those [husbands] are not the best of you.

Ibn Hanbal (No. 7396)

49

As the woman's right to decide about her marriage is recognized, so also is her right to seek an end for an unsuccessful marriage. To provide for the stability of the family, however, and in order to protect it from hasty decisions under temporary emotional stress, certain steps and waiting periods should be observed by men and women seeking divorce. Considering the relatively more emotional nature of women, a good reason for asking for divorce should be brought before the judge. Like a man, however, a woman can divorce her husband without resorting to the court, if the nuptial contract allows that. More specifically, some aspects of Islamic Law concerning marriage and divorce are interesting and are worthy of separate treatment.[21] When the continuation of the marriage relationship is impossible for any reason, men are still taught to seek a gracious end for it. The Qur'an states the following about such cases.

﴿وَإِذَا طَلَّقْتُمُ ٱلنِّسَآءَ فَبَلَغْنَ أَجَلَهُنَّ فَأَمْسِكُوهُنَّ بِمَعْرُوفٍ أَوْ سَرِّحُوهُنَّ بِمَعْرُوفٍ وَلَا تُمْسِكُوهُنَّ ضِرَارًا لِّتَعْتَدُواْ﴾

---

21 A separate paper clarifying the position of Islam with regard to polygamy (polygyny) is available from The MSA Islamic Book Service, PO Box 38, Plainfield, IN 46168 (USA). It is sufficient to say here that polygamy existed in almost all nations and was even sanctioned by Judaism and Christianity until recent centuries. The *Qur'an* is the only revealed scripture that explicitly limited polygamy and discouraged its practice by various stringent conditions. One reason for not categorically forbidding polygamy is that in different places at different times, there may exist individual or social exigencies that make polygamy a better solution than either divorce or a hypocritical monogamy while indulging in all types of illicit relations.

50

When you divorce women, and they reach their prescribed term, then retain them in kindness and retain them not for injury so that you transgress [the limits].

Qur'an (2:231); see also *Qur'an* 2:229 and 33:49

As a mother:

Islam considers kindness to parents next to the worship of God, as the following verse from the *Qur'an* shows.

﴿وَوَصَّيْنَا ٱلْإِنسَٰنَ بِوَٰلِدَيْهِ حَمَلَتْهُ أُمُّهُ وَهْنًا عَلَىٰ وَهْنٍ﴾

And we have enjoined upon man [to be good] to his parents: His mother bears him in weakness upon weakness. . .

Qur'an (31:14); see also *Qur'an* 46:15, 29:8

Moreover, the *Qur'an* has a special recommendation for the good treatment of mothers:

﴿ ❋ وَقَضَىٰ رَبُّكَ أَلَّا تَعْبُدُوٓا۟ إِلَّآ إِيَّاهُ وَبِٱلْوَٰلِدَيْنِ إِحْسَٰنًا﴾

Your Lord has decreed that you worship none save Him, and that you be kind to your parents . . .

Qur'an (17:23)

A man came to Prophet Muhammad (Peace be upon him) asking:

51

O Messenger of God, who among the people is the most worthy of my good company? The Prophet (Peace be upon him) said, 'Your mother'. The man said, 'Then who else?'. The Prophet (Peace be upon him) said, 'Your mother' The man asked 'Then who else?'. The Prophet (Peace be upon him) said, 'Your mother'. The man asked 'Then who else?' Only then did the Prophet (Peace be upon him) say, 'Your father.'

Al-Bukhari and Muslim.

A famous saying of the Prophet is

Paradise is at the feet of mothers . . . It is the generous . . . [in character] who is good to women, and it is the wicked who insults them.

In *Al-Nisa'i, Ibn-Majah, Ahmad*

The economic aspect

Islam decreed a right of which women were deprived – the right of independent ownership. That right is not yet fully realized in the West, even as late as this century.[22] According to Islamic Law, the woman's right to her money, real estate or other properties is fully acknowledged. This right undergoes no change whether she is single or married. She retains her full rights to buy, sell, mortgage or lease any or all her properties. It is nowhere suggested in the Law that a woman is a minor simply because she is a female. It is also noteworthy that such

---

22 For example, it was not until 1938 that the French Law was amended so as to recognize the eligibility of women to contract. A married woman, however, was still required to secure her husband's permission before she could dispense with her private property. See for example al-Siba'i, *Al-Mar'ah bayna al-Fiqh wa al-Qanun*, pp. 31–37.

right applies to her properties before marriage as well as to whatever she acquires thereafter.

With regard to the woman's right to seek employment it should be stated first that Islam regards her role in society as a mother and a wife as the most sacred and essential role. Neither maids nor babysitters can possibly take the mother's place as the educator of upright, complex-free, and carefully reared children. Such a noble and vital role, which largely shapes the future of nations, cannot be regarded as 'idleness'.

However, there is no decree in Islam that forbids women from seeking employment whenever there is a necessity for it, especially in positions that fit their nature and in which society needs them most. Examples of these professions are nursing, teaching (especially for children) and medicine. Moreover, there is no restriction on benefiting from women's exceptional talent in any field. Even for the position of a judge, where there may be a tendency to doubt the woman's fitness for the post due to her more emotional nature, we find early Muslim scholars such as *Abu-Hanifa* and *al-Tabary* holding that there is nothing wrong with it. In addition, Islam restored to women the right of inheritance, after they themselves were an object of inheritance in some cultures. A woman's share is completely hers and no one can make any claim on it, including her father and her husband, as the following verse from the *Qur'an* shows.

﷽ لِّلرِّجَالِ نَصِيبٌ مِّمَّا تَرَكَ ٱلْوَٰلِدَانِ وَٱلْأَقْرَبُونَ وَلِلنِّسَآءِ نَصِيبٌ مِّمَّا تَرَكَ ٱلْوَٰلِدَانِ وَٱلْأَقْرَبُونَ مِمَّا قَلَّ مِنْهُ أَوْ كَثُرَ نَصِيبًا مَّفْرُوضًا ۝

Unto men [of the family] belongs a share of that which parents and near kindred leave, and unto women a share of that which parents and near kindred leave, whether it be a little or much – a determinate share.

Qur'an (4:7)

The woman's share in most cases is one-half the man's share, with no implication that she is worth half a man! It would seem grossly inconsistent after the overwhelming evidence of women's equitable treatment in Islam, discussed in the preceding pages, to make such an inference. This variation in inheritance rights is only consistent with the variations in financial responsibilities of men and women according to the Islamic Law. Man in Islam is fully responsible for the maintenance of his wife, his children and in some cases of his needy relatives – especially the females. This responsibility is neither waived nor reduced because of his wife's wealth or because of her access to any personal income gained from work, rent, profit or any other legal means.

A woman, on the other hand, is far more secure financially and is far less burdened with any claims on her possessions. Her possessions before marriage do not transfer to her husband and she even keeps her maiden name. She has no obligation to spend on her family out of such properties or out of her income after marriage. She is entitled to the *Mahr*, which she takes from her husband at the time of marriage. If she is divorced, she may get an alimony from her ex-husband.

An examination of the inheritance law within the

overall framework of the Islamic Law reveals not only justice but also an abundance of compassion for women[23].

The political aspect

Any fair investigation of the teachings of Islam or into the history of the Islamic civilization will surely find clear evidence of women's equality with men in what we call today 'political rights'. This includes the right of election as well as the nomination to political offices. It also includes women's right to participate in public affairs. Both in the *Qur'an* and in Islamic history we find examples of women who participated in serious discussions and who even argued with the Prophet (Peace be upon him) himself (see *Qur'an* 58:14 and 60:10–12).

During the Caliphate of *Omar Ibn al-Khattab*, a woman argued with him in the mosque, proved her point and caused him to declare in the presence of people: 'A woman is right and Omar is wrong.'

Although not mentioned in the *Qur'an*, one *Hadith* of the Prophet is interpreted to make women ineligible for the position of head of state. The *Hadith* referred to is, roughly translated: 'A people will not prosper if they let a woman be their leader.' This limitation, however, has nothing to do with the dignity of women nor with their rights. Rather, it is related to the natural differences in the

---

23 For a good discussion of this point, also for the acceptance of women's witness according to Islamic Law, see *Abd al-Ati, Hamudah, Islam in Focus*, pp. 117–118 and *Mustafa al-Siba'i, Al-Mar'ah bayn al-Fiqh wa al-Qanun* (in Arabic) pp. 21–37.

biological and psychological make-up of men and women.

According to Islam, the head of the state is no mere figure-head. He leads people in prayers, especially on Fridays and festivities; and he is continuously engaged in the process of decision-making pertaining to the security and well-being of his people. This demanding position, or any similar one such as Commander of the Army, is generally inconsistent with the physiological and psychological make-up of women in general. It is a medical fact that during their monthly periods and during pregnancy, women undergo various physiological and psychological changes. Such changes may occur during an emergency situation, thus affecting their decisions, without considering the excessive strain that is produced. Moreover, some decisions require a maximum of rationality and a minimum of emotionality – a requirement that does not coincide with the instinctive nature of women.

Even in modern times, and even in the most developed countries, it is rare to find a woman in the position of a head of state acting as more than a figure-head, a woman commander of the Armed Services, or even a proportionate number of women representatives in parliaments or similar bodies. One cannot possibly ascribe this to backwardness of various nations or to any constitutional limitation on women's rights to be in such a position as a head of state or as a member of parliament. It is more logical to explain the present situation in terms of the natural and indisputable differences between men and women – differences that do not imply any 'supremacy' of one over the other. Rather, these differences imply the 'complementary' roles in life of both sexes.

Such deviations were unfairly exaggerated by some writers. The worst of these were superficially taken by the Western reader to represent the teachings of 'Islam' without making any original and unbiased study of the authentic sources of these teachings. Even with such deviations, three facts – outlined below – are worth mentioning.

1 The history of Muslims is rich with women of great achievements in all walks of life from as early as the seventh century.[24]

2 It is impossible for anyone to justify any mistreatment of women by any decree of rule embodied in the Islamic Law; nor could anyone dare to cancel, reduce or distort the clear-cut legal rights of women that are given in Islamic Law.

3 Throughout history, the reputation, chastity and maternal role of Muslim women were objects of admiration by impartial observers.

It is also worthwhile stating that the status which women reached during the present era was not achieved by the kindness of men or by natural progress. Rather, it was achieved through a long struggle and sacrifice on women's part, and only when society needed their contribution and

---

24 See for example, A. Sulaiman Nadvi, *Heroic Deeds of Muslim Women*, Islamic Publication Ltd., Lahore, Pakistan. See also Siddiqi, *Women in Islam*, Institute of Islamic Culture, Lahore, Pakistan, 1959.

work – especially during the two world wars, and after the rapid increase in technology.

In the case of Islam, such compassionate and dignified status was decreed, not because it reflects the environment of the seventh century, nor under the threat or pressure of women and their organizations, but rather because of its intrinsic truthfulness. If this indicates anything, it would demonstrate the divine origin of the *Qur'an* and the truthfulness of the message of Islam which, unlike human philosophies and ideologies, was far from proceeding from its human environment. It is a message that established such humane principles that neither grew obsolete during the course of time after the passage of many centuries, nor can become obsolete in the future. After all, this is the message of the All-Wise and All-Knowing God whose wisdom and knowledge go beyond the limits of human thought and progress.

Islam is a practical way of life, dealing with all aspects of human civilization. Islam allows restricted polygamy-marriage to more than one woman. The normal Muslim practice is monogamy – one man married to one woman.

Polygamy is the exception

Muslim men are only allowed to marry more than one woman if, and only if, they are prepared to and are capable of dealing equally and justly with each of their wives. This fact is emphasized in the following verses from the Holy *Qur'an* (4:2–3).

To orphans restore their property
(When they reach their age).
Nor substitute (your) worthless things
For (their) good ones; and devour not
Their substance (by mixing it up)
With your own. For this is
Indeed a great sin.
If you fear that you shall not
Be able to deal justly
With the orphans,
Marry women of your choice,
Two, or three or four;
But if you feel that you shall not
Be able to deal justly (with them),
Then only one, or
That your right hands possess.
That will be more suitable,
To prevent you
From doing injustice
Qur'an (4:2–3)

﴿وَءَاتُواْ ٱلۡيَتَٰمَىٰٓ أَمۡوَٰلَهُمۡۖ وَلَا

تَتَبَدَّلُواْ ٱلۡخَبِيثَ بِٱلطَّيِّبِۖ وَلَا

تَأۡكُلُوٓاْ أَمۡوَٰلَهُمۡ إِلَىٰٓ أَمۡوَٰلِكُمۡۚ

إِنَّهُۥ كَانَ حُوبًا كَبِيرًا ٢ وَإِنۡ

خِفۡتُمۡ أَلَّا تُقۡسِطُواْ فِى ٱلۡيَتَٰمَىٰ

فَٱنكِحُواْ مَا طَابَ لَكُم مِّنَ

ٱلنِّسَآءِ مَثۡنَىٰ وَثُلَٰثَ وَرُبَٰعَۖ فَإِنۡ

خِفۡتُمۡ أَلَّا تَعۡدِلُواْ فَوَٰحِدَةً أَوۡ مَا

مَلَكَتۡ أَيۡمَٰنُكُمۡۚ ذَٰلِكَ أَدۡنَىٰٓ أَلَّا

تَعُولُواْ ٣ ﴾

As Islam prohibits adultery and the keeping of mistresses, a man may marry again as a result of special conditions, such as the ones listed below.

● When a wife is barren and cannot bear children. It is better for the man to have a second wife rather than divorce the first.

● If the wife is chronically ill and unable to carry out her normal marital duties, then the husband may marry a second wife.

● Polygamy may be an answer to a society that has more women than men. This happens especially after wars.

Nevertheless, in Islam it is considered morally desirable to obtain the consent of the first wife.

An overwhelming majority of Muslims are monogamous – they have only one wife. The fact that a minority of Muslims have more than one wife has become a centre of propaganda against Islamic teachings and undoubtedly such emphasis on a very minor issue can give a misleading impression of the true Islamic way of life.

Prohibition in Islam

The Prohibition of Things is Due to Their Impurity and Harmfulness. It is the right of God, the One who created the universe and bestowed innumerable favours upon mankind, to legalize or prohibit as He deems proper.

In Islam things are prohibited only because they are impure or harmful. If something is entirely harmful it is 'haram', and if it is entirely beneficial it is 'halal'; if the harm of it outweighs its benefit it is *haram*, while if its benefit outweighs its harm it is *halal*. This principle is explained in the *Qur'an* in relation to wine and gambling.

They ask you concerning

Wine and gambling.

Say (O Prophet); In them

Is great sin and some benefit

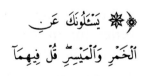

For human beings, but the sin is
Greater than the benefit ...
Qur'an (2:219)

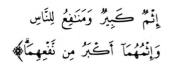

Another Islamic principle is that if something is prohibited, anything that leads to it is likewise prohibited. By this means Islam intends to block all avenues leading to what is *haram*. For example, Islam has prohibited adultery; it has also prohibited anything that leads to it or makes it attractive such as seductive clothing, private meetings and casual meetings between men and women, the depiction of nudity, pornographic literature, obscene songs and so on.

One of the beauties of Islam is that it has prohibited only such things that are unnecessary and dispensable, while providing alternatives that are better, and which give greater ease and comfort to human beings.

Allah has prohibited seeking omens by drawing lots but has provided the alternative of *istikhara*, which is to ask guidance from Him in making a choice between two conflicting choices. He has prohibited usury but has encouraged profitable trade. He has prohibited gambling but has encouraged healthy forms of competition such as sports. He has prohibited adultery, fornication and homosexuality but has encouraged lawful marriage.

He has prohibited intoxicating drinks in order that people may enjoy other delicious drinks that are beneficial for the body and mind. And He has prohibited unclean food but provides alternative wholesome food.

61

O you who believe!
Do not make unlawful
The good things which God
Has made lawful for you.
But commit no excess
For God does not Love
Those given to excess.

Qur'an (5:87)

Pork

Forbidden by God's order in the Holy Qur'an:

﴿ يَـٰٓأَيُّهَا ٱلَّذِينَ ءَامَنُوا۟ لَا تُحَرِّمُوا۟ طَيِّبَـٰتِ مَآ أَحَلَّ ٱللَّهُ لَكُمْ وَلَا تَعْتَدُوٓا۟ إِنَّ ٱللَّهَ لَا يُحِبُّ ٱلْمُعْتَدِينَ ﴿٨٧﴾ ﴾

Forbidden to you (for food),
Are dead meat, blood, the
Flesh of swine, and that on
Which has been invoked,
The name of other than God. . .

Qur'an (5:3)

﴿ حُرِّمَتْ عَلَيْكُمُ ٱلْمَيْتَةُ وَٱلدَّمُ وَلَحْمُ ٱلْخِنزِيرِ وَمَآ أُهِلَّ لِغَيْرِ ٱللَّهِ بِهِۦ ﴾

Forbidden in the Holy Bible:

And the swine . . . he is unclean to you. Of the flesh shall ye not eat, and their carcase shall ye not touch; they are unclean to you.

Leviticus (11:7–8)

The same command is repeated in Deuteronomy, 14:8 and similarly in Matthew, 5:17–19.

Forbidden from the medical point of view:

● Herbivorous animals such as cattle and sheep eat of clean fresh fodder and cereals, whereas the pig will eat waste animal products, including offal and carrion and even human flesh.

● Worms and parasites are transferred from pig to man. They include Trichina Worms, Tapeworms (Taenia Solium), Roundworms, Hookworms, Faciolopsis Buski, Paragonimius Clonorchis Sinosis, and Erysipelothrix Rhusiophathiae. These worms and parasites are responsible for many diseases; many of them are contagious, others are fatal. This includes anaemia, inflammation of the bowels, pneumonia, and serious diseases of the liver and chest region.

● Uric acid (known cause of heart disease and rheumatism) approximately has a 20 per cent extraction rate from the kidneys of the pig. Herbivorous animals have an 80 per cent extraction rate. Hence, relative to other animals, a high concentration of uric acid is found in pork.

● Fatty acids. Pork fat is very harmful to the body because it is difficult to digest and to efficiently convert to energy. Pork fat is absorbed by the body and consequently accumulates in human tissue as animal fat. Herbivorous animal fat is broken down by the body within the bloodstream resynthesizing the fat into a readily available energy source.

Note

Pork is not the only meat that is prohibited; the flesh of all carnivorous animals is not allowed to be eaten, while that of herbivorous animals is permitted.

Halal meat

Conditions for lawful slaughtering are the Declaration of the Name of God before Slaughtering and the wisdom of the Islamic method of slaughtering.

The Declaration of the Name of GOD before Slaughteging

﴿فَكُلُواْ مِمَّا ذُكِرَ ٱسْمُ ٱللَّهِ عَلَيْهِ إِن

Then eat of that over which

The name of Allah has been
كُنتُم بِـَٔايَـٰتِهِۦ مُؤْمِنِينَ ۝﴾

Mentioned, If you believe in His Signs.

Qur'an (6:118)
﴿وَلَا تَأْكُلُواْ مِمَّا

لَمْ يُذْكَرِ ٱسْمُ ٱللَّهِ عَلَيْهِ وَإِنَّهُۥ لَفِسْقٌ

And do not eat of that

Over which the name of
وَإِنَّ ٱلشَّيَـٰطِينَ لَيُوحُونَ إِلَىٰٓ أَوْلِيَآئِهِمْ

Allah has not been mentioned,

For truly that is impiety . . .
لِيُجَـٰدِلُوكُمْ وَإِنْ أَطَعْتُمُوهُمْ

Qur'an (6:121)
إِنَّكُمْ لَمُشْرِكُونَ ۝﴾

The wisdom of the Islamic method of slaughtering

The wisdom of the Islamic method of slaughtering is to take the animal's life in the quickest and least painful way; the requirements of using a sharp instrument and of cutting the throat relate to this end. By using a sharp knife and cutting the windpipe, the gullet and the two jugular veins without severing the spine, the animal will be subject to the least amount of pain. This method allows the animal's heart to pump out blood, while the brain is supplied with blood, instructing the heart to beat.

Health-wise, such a method is justified as it allows the minimum amount of blood to remain in the flesh. In this way the high level of uric acid found in the bloodstream is kept to a minimum. It is a known medical fact that uric acid is responsible for most cases of heart disease and rheumatism.

The Islamic method of slaughter is ordered by God and it is obvious from a medical point of view that such a way is most beneficial for the health of humans.

What about food?

Although much simpler than the dietary law followed by Jews and the early Christians, the code that Muslims observe forbids the consumption of blood, pork and any kind of intoxicating substances. The Prophet taught that 'your body has rights over you', and the consumption of wholesome food and the leading of a healthy lifestyle are seen as religious obligations.

The Prophet (Peace be upon him) said: 'Ask God for certainty [of faith] and well-being; for after certainty, no one is given any gift better than health!'

Tolerance in Islam

Does Islam tolerate other beliefs?

The Qur'an says:

Allah does not forbid you with regards to those who do not fight you for [your] faith nor drive you out of your homes, from dealing kindly and justly with them; for Allah loves those who are just.

Qur'an (60:8)

It is one function of Islamic law to protect the privileged status of minorities, and this is why non-Muslim places of worship have flourished all over the Islamic world. History provides many examples of Muslim tolerance towards other faiths: when the Caliph Omar entered Jerusalem in the year 634, Islam granted freedom of worship to all religious communities in the city.

Islamic law also permits non-Muslim minorities to set up their own courts, which implement family laws drawn up by the minorities themselves.

What do Muslims think about Jesus?

Muslims respect and revere Jesus (Peace be upon him), and await his Second Coming. They consider him one of the greatest of God's messengers to mankind. The *Qur'an* confirms his virgin birth (there is a chapter of the *Qur'an* entitled 'Mary'), and Mary is considered the purest woman in all creation. The *Qur'an* describes the Annunciation as follows.

'Behold!' the Angel said, 'God has chosen you, and purified you, and chosen you above the women of all nations. O Mary, God gives you good news of a word from Him, whose name shall be the Messiah, Jesus son of Mary, honoured in this world and the Hereafter, and one of those brought near to God. He shall speak to the people from his cradle and in maturity, and shall be of the righteous.'

She said: 'O my Lord! How shall I have a son when no man has touched me?' He said: 'Even so; Allah creates whatever He wills. When He decrees a thing, He says to it, "Be!" and it is.'

Qur'an (3:42–7)

Jesus (Peace be upon him) was born miraculously through the same power which had brought Adam (Peace be upon him) into being without a father.

Truly, the likeness of Jesus with God is as the likeness of Adam. He created him of dust, and then said to him, 'Be!' and he was.

Qur'an (3:59)

During his prophetic mission Jesus (Peace be upon him) performed many miracles. The *Qur'an* tells us that he said:

I have come to you with a sign from your Lord: I make for you out of day, the figure of a bird, and breathe into it and it becomes a bird by Allah's leave. And I heal the blind, and the lepers, and I raise the dead by Allah's leave.

Qur'an (3:49)

Neither Muhammad (Peace be upon him) nor Jesus (Peace be upon him) came to change the basic doctrine of the belief in One God, brought by earlier prophets, but to confirm and renew it. In the *Qur'an* Jesus (Peace be upon him) is reported as saying that he came:

... to attest the law which was before me. And to make lawful to you part of what was forbidden you; I have come to you with a sign from your Lord, so fear Allah and 'obey Me'.

Qur'an (3:50)

The Prophet Muhammad (Peace be upon him) said:

Whoever believes there is no god but God, alone without

partner, that Muhammad (Peace be upon him) is His Messenger, that Jesus is the servant and Mesenger of God, His word breathed into Mary and a spirit from Him, and that Paradise and Hell are true, shall be received by Allah into Heaven.

Hadith from Bukhari

Jesus (Peace be upon him) in the *Qur'an*

The acceptance of Jesus Christ (Peace be upon him) by Muslims is a fundamental article of faith in Islam, and a Muslim can never think of Jesus (Peace be upon him) in any derogatory terms. A Muslim is prohibited from defaming Jesus (Peace be upon him) or any other prophet of God.

A Muslim's concept of God, religion, prophethood, revelation and humanity makes him accept Jesus (Peace be upon him) not only as a historical fact but also as one of the most distinguished Apostles of God. Islamic beliefs depict Jesus (Peace be upon him) in a most respectful manner and place him as high in status as God himself has placed him. The Muslim believes that the greatness of Jesus (Peace be upon him) arises from the fact that he was chosen by God and honoured him with His word; that he was entrusted with the revelations of God and commissioned to teach His message, that he was a prophet of character and personality, that he was sincere inwardly, that he fought hypocrisy and blasphemy, that he was distinguished in the beginning at the time of his birth and in the end at the time of his ascension, and that he was a sign to the people and a mercy from God.

In fact, Mary (Peace be upon her) is the only woman mentioned in the *Qur'an* by name.

Jesus in the *Qur'an*:

Below are some verses from the *Qur'an* that relate to the birth of Jesus.

Behold! the angels said;
O Mary! God gives
Glad tidings of a Word
From Him; his name
Will be Christ Jesus.
The son of Mary, held in honour
In this world and the Hereafter
And of (the company of) those
Nearest to God:
Qur'an (3:45)

﴿إِذْ قَالَتِ ٱلْمَلَٰٓئِكَةُ يَٰمَرْيَمُ إِنَّ ٱللَّهَ يُبَشِّرُكِ بِكَلِمَةٍ مِّنْهُ ٱسْمُهُ ٱلْمَسِيحُ عِيسَى ٱبْنُ مَرْيَمَ وَجِيهًا فِى ٱلدُّنْيَا وَٱلْءَاخِرَةِ وَمِنَ ٱلْمُقَرَّبِينَ ﴿٤٥﴾﴾

She said: O My Lord!
How shall I have a son
When no man has touched me?
He said: Even so;
God creates
What He wills
When He has decreed
A plan, He but says
To it, 'Be' and it is!.
Qur'an (3:47)

﴿قَالَتْ رَبِّ أَنَّىٰ يَكُونُ لِى وَلَدٌ وَلَمْ يَمْسَسْنِى بَشَرٌ قَالَ كَذَٰلِكِ ٱللَّهُ يَخْلُقُ مَا يَشَآءُ إِذَا قَضَىٰ أَمْرًا فَإِنَّمَا يَقُولُ لَهُ كُن فَيَكُونُ ﴿٤٧﴾﴾

And God will teach him
The Book of Wisdom,
The Law and the Gospel.
Qur'an (3:48)

﴿وَيُعَلِّمُهُ ٱلْكِتَٰبَ وَٱلْحِكْمَةَ

وَٱلتَّوْرَىٰةَ وَٱلْإِنجِيلَ ٤٨﴾

The similitude of Jesus
Before God is as that of Adam;
He created him from dust,
Then said to him, 'Be',
And he was.
Qur'an (3:59)

﴿إِنَّ مَثَلَ عِيسَىٰ عِندَ ٱللَّهِ

كَمَثَلِ ءَادَمَ خَلَقَهُ مِن تُرَابٍ

ثُمَّ قَالَ لَهُ كُن فَيَكُونُ ٥٩﴾

Second Coming of Jesus

As has been revealed in the Holy *Qur'an* 'Jesus Christ
(Peace be upon him) will be returning to this world before
the Day of Resurrection to become a leader of the Muslim
Nation'.

And [Jesus] shall be
A Sign [for the coming of]
The Hour of [Judgement]
Therefore have no doubt
About the [Hour], but
Follow ye Me;
This is a straight way''.
Qur'an (43:61)

﴿وَإِنَّهُ لَعِلْمٌ لِّلسَّاعَةِ فَلَا

تَمْتَرُنَّ بِهَا وَٱتَّبِعُونِ هَٰذَا

صِرَٰطٌ مُّسْتَقِيمٌ ٦١﴾

70

Let not the Evil One
Hinder you for he is
To you a plain enemy.
Qur'an (43:62)

﴿وَلَا يَصُدَّنَّكُمُ ٱلشَّيْطَانُ إِنَّهُ
لَكُمْ عَدُوٌّ مُّبِينٌ ۝﴾

And when Jesus came
To you with clear signs he said
I have come to you with Wisdom
And in Order to make clear
To you some of the points
In which you differ therefore
Fear God and obey me.
Qur'an (43:63)

﴿وَلَمَّا جَاءَ عِيسَىٰ بِٱلْبَيِّنَاتِ قَالَ
قَدْ جِئْتُكُم بِٱلْحِكْمَةِ وَلِأُبَيِّنَ
لَكُم بَعْضَ ٱلَّذِى تَخْتَلِفُونَ فِيهِ
فَٱتَّقُوا ٱللَّهَ وَأَطِيعُونِ ۝﴾

For God, He is my Lord
And your Lord: so worship Him.
This is a straight way.
Qur'an (43:64)

﴿إِنَّ ٱللَّهَ هُوَ رَبِّى وَرَبُّكُمْ
فَٱعْبُدُوهُ هَٰذَا صِرَٰطٌ
مُّسْتَقِيمٌ ۝﴾

Reproduced below are verses 119 to 120; Maida, Chapter
5, depicting the scene of Judgement Day, when God will
question Jesus (Peace be upon him) regarding the
misdirected zeal of his supposed followers in worshipping
him and his mother, and his response.

قَالَ اللَّهُ هَذَا يَوْمُ يَنفَعُ الصَّادِقِينَ صِدْقُهُمْ لَهُمْ جَنَّاتٌ تَجْرِى مِن تَحْتِهَا الْأَنْهَارُ

خَالِدِينَ فِيهَا أَبَدًا رَّضِىَ اللَّهُ عَنْهُمْ وَرَضُوا عَنْهُ ذَلِكَ الْفَوْزُ الْعَظِيمُ ۱۱۹ لِلَّهِ مُلْكُ

السَّمَوَاتِ وَالْأَرْضِ وَمَا فِيهِنَّ وَهُوَ عَلَى كُلِّ شَىْءٍ قَدِيرٌ ۱۲۰

And Behold! God will say:
O Jesus the son of Mary!
Did you say unto men,
Worship me and my mother
As gods in derogation of God?
He will say: Glory to Thee!
Never could I say
What I had no right [to say].
Had I said
Such a thing. You would
Indeed have known it.
You know what is
In my heart, though I
Know not what is
In thine. For You
Know in full
All that is hidden.
Qur'an (5:116)

وَإِذْ قَالَ اللَّهُ يَـٰعِيسَى ابْنَ

مَرْيَمَ ءَأَنتَ قُلْتَ لِلنَّاسِ

اتَّخِذُونِي وَأُمِّيَ إِلَـٰهَيْنِ مِن

دُونِ اللَّهِ قَالَ سُبْحَـٰنَكَ مَا

يَكُونُ لِي أَنْ أَقُولَ مَا لَيْسَ لِي

بِحَقٍّ إِن كُنتُ قُلْتُهُ فَقَدْ

عَلِمْتَهُ تَعْلَمُ مَا فِي نَفْسِى

وَلَا أَعْلَمُ مَا فِي نَفْسِكَ إِنَّكَ

أَنتَ عَلَّامُ الْغُيُوبِ ۱۱۶

Never said I to them
Anything except what You
Did command me
To say; Worship
God, my Lord and your Lord.
And I was a witness
Over them whilst I dwelled
Amongst them; when You
Did take me up.
You were the Watcher
Over them, and You
Are a witness to all things.
Qur'an (5:117)

﴿مَا قُلْتُ لَهُمْ إِلَّا مَآ أَمَرْتَنِي بِهِۦٓ

أَنِ ٱعْبُدُواْ ٱللَّهَ رَبِّي وَرَبَّكُمْ

وَكُنتُ عَلَيْهِمْ شَهِيدًا مَّا دُمْتُ

فِيهِمْ فَلَمَّا تَوَفَّيْتَنِي كُنتَ أَنتَ

ٱلرَّقِيبَ عَلَيْهِمْ وَأَنتَ عَلَىٰ كُلِّ

شَىْءٍ شَهِيدٌ ۝١١٧﴾

If You do punish them,
They are Your servants:
If You do forgive them,
You are the Exalted in power,
The wise.
Qur'an (5:118)

﴿إِن تُعَذِّبْهُمْ فَإِنَّهُمْ عِبَادُكَ وَإِن

تَغْفِرْ لَهُمْ فَإِنَّكَ أَنتَ ٱلْعَزِيزُ

ٱلْحَكِيمُ ۝١١٨﴾

Prophet Muhammad (Peace be upon him) in the Old and New Testaments

The Old Testament

Below are three extracts from the Old Testament that make reference to the Prophet Muhammad (Peace be upon him).

He saw two riders one of them was a rider upon an ass and the other a rider upon a camel, he hearkened diligently with much heed.

Isaiah (XXI:7)

Isaiah saw two riders in a vision, one of them was a rider upon an ass and the other a rider upon a camel. In our opinion the above passage is the faithful rendering of the original Hebrew. In the English Bible, however, it is translated as: 'He saw a chariot of asses and a chariot of camels', and so on.

The Vulgate has it as follows: 'He saw a chariot of two horsemen, a rider upon an ass and a rider upon a camel', and so on.

There can be no doubt that of the two riders represented by the Prophet Isaiah as being the restorers of the true worship of the God-head, the rider of the ass is Jesus Christ (Peace be upon him), because that's how he made his entry into Jerusalem. The rider of the camel is meant to be the Prophet of Arabia, Arabia being a country where the camel is characteristic of conveyance.

His mouth is most sweet; yea, he is Muhammad altogether lovely. This is my beloved and this is my friend. O daughter of

Jerusalem.

Song of Solomon (5:16)

King Solomon has named the Prophet that was to come 'Muhammadin.' In Hebrew the suffix is used to express respect as the term 'Eloha', which means 'God', and is mentioned in the Bible as 'Elohim.' It is thus clear that Solomon has quite distinctly mentioned the name of the Prophet that was to come as 'Muhamma'. But an error is made, intentionally or un-intentionally, by translation of the proper name as 'Altogether Lovely'. Even the translation 'Altogether Lovely' is a befitting attribute of the Holy Prophet, as mentioned in the words of *Hadith*.

The Lord thy God will raise unto thee a Prophet from the midst of thee, of thy brethren, like unto Me; unto him ye shall hearken.

Deuteronomy (18:15)

The New Testament

Below are several extracts from the New Testament that make clear reference to the Prophet Muhammad (Peace be upon him).

The Gospel of Barnabas

Here we see the prophecies and glad tidings relating to the advent of the Last Prophet Muhammad (Peace be upon him) as foretold in the Gospel of Barnabas, which was accepted as a canonical gospel in the churches of Alexandria until AD325 In AD383 the Pope acquired a copy of the Gospel which was put in his private library. When Pope Sixtos IX (1565–1590) became the pope, his friend Fra Marine saw the Gospel of Barnabas there. He translated it into the Italian language, his mother tongue.

The Italian manuscript was discovered by J. F. Cramer, Counsellor to the King of Prussia, who, in 1713, presented it to Prince Eugene of Savoy. In 1738, along with the library of the Prince, it found its way into Hofbiblyothex in Vienna. The manuscript in the Imperial Library of Vienna is still there. This was translated into English by Mr and Mrs Ragg in Oxford, in 1907 and printed in Oxford by the Clarendon Press.

Barnabas was a Jew born in Cyprus. His name was Joses, and due to his piety and devotion, he was given the title of Barnabas by other Apostles. In the Acts of the Apostles, Barnabas is mentioned as follows.

And Joses, who by the Apostles was surnamed Barnabas, which is being interpreted [the son of Consolation], a Levite and of the country of Cyprus

Barnabas understood the teachings of Christ better as a result of his close association with Jesus (Peace be upon him). The advent of Prophet Muhammad (Peace be upon him) follows here as foretold by Jesus Christ (Peace be upon him).

Then said the Priest,

How shall the Comforter be called

And what sign shall reveal his coming?

Jesus (Peace be upon him) answered:

The name of the Comforter is Admirable

For God gave him the name

When He had created his Soul,

And placed it in Celestial Splendour.

God said: Await Muhammad,

For thy sake I will create

Paradise, the World, and
A great multitude of creatures.
Whereof I make thee a present.
Insomuch that whoso
Shall bless thee shall be blessed,
And whoso shall curse thee
Shall be accursed.
When I shall send thee unto
The world, I shall send thee
As my Messenger of Salvation,
And thy word shall be true.
Insomuch that Heaven and Earth
Shall fail,
But thy faith shall never fail.
Muhammad is his blessed name.
Then the crowd lifted up
Their voice saying:
'O God, send us Thy Messenger.
O Muhammad, come quickly for
The salvation of the world.'

I therefore say unto you that Messenger of God is a splendour
that shall give gladness to nearly all that God hath made, for
he is adorned with the spirit of Understanding and Counsel,
the spirit of Wisdom and Might, the spirit of Fear and Love,
the spirit of Prudence and Temperance: he is adorned with
the spirit of Charity and Mercy, the spirit of Justice and Piety,
the spirit of Gentleness and Patience, which he had received
from God three times more than he had given to all his
creatures. O blessed time, when he shall come to the world.

Believe me that I have seen him and have done him reverence, even as every prophet hath seen him: seeing that of his spirit God giveth to them prophecy. And when I saw him my soul was filled with consolation, saying: O Muhammad, God be with thee, and may He make me worthy to untie thy shoelace, for obtaining this I shall be a great prophet and holy one of God.

This, now, is a fascinating revelation of the private teachings not yet divulged to the masses. The purity of the character of Jesus (Peace be upon him) gives boundless charm to the magnificence of a God-given wisdom unto Christ (Peace be upon him).

The Sacrifice of Ishmael together with the further evidence of the Prophecy of Christ (Peace be upon him) in the matter of the advent of the Prophet Muhammad (Peace be upon him) has been hidden behind a 'veil' – a veil that is intermingled with strange interpretations of the present day. This remains as a plain and simple truth without the 'touch of allegory'. It is not susceptible to several interpretations. It gives the heretofore veiled incidents of the life of Christ (Peace be upon him). The untold secrets now remain for the public.

It is for any challenger of facts to disprove that these amazing documents of Barnabas are not in the Imperial Library in Vienna. The root for the liberty of our soul, planted in the heart of the earth by Saint Barnabas, is that he instinctively Dispensed the knowledge gained to the Disciples to convey and carry throughout the ages.

During the early ministry of Christ (Peace be upon him) he sought, trained and prepared twelve disciples, among whom was Barnabas, to be spiritually worthy and morally qualified, to perpetuate the knowledge that Christ Jesus (Peace be upon him) brought to earth. The exclusion of these secrets during the Christian era is a demonstration of a knowledge, which could become the most potent and powerful influence for the well-being and happiness of the nations. It could prove to be the process of gradual elimination of national and international wars and strifes, that saves humanity from error and sin – an attempt that is the mother of the improvement of mankind.

I have yet many things to say unto you, but ye cannot bear them now. How be it when he, the spirit of truth is come, he will guide you into all truth; for he shall speak of himself, but whatsoever he shall hear, that shall he speak and he will show you things to come.

John 16:12–3

Biblical verses testify Jesus (Peace be upon him) is not God

Ye men of Israel, hear these words: Jesus (Peace be upon him) of Nazareth, a man approved by God among you by miracles and wonder and signs, which God did by him in the midst of you as ye yourselves also know.

Acts (21:22)

And I fell at his feet to worship him. And he said unto me, see thou do it not: I am thy fellow servant, and of thy brethren that have testimony of Jesus (Peace be upon him): Worship God.

Revelations (19:10)

For have I not spoken of myself: But the Father which sent me. He gave a commandment, what I should say, and what I should speak.

John (12:29)

I can of my own self do nothing: As I hear I judge: And my judgement is just: Because I seek not my own will, but the will of the Father which have sent me. If I bear witness of myself, my witness is not true.

John (5:20-31)

. . . for my Father is greater than I.

John (14:28)

Verily, verily, I say unto you, the servant is no greater than his Lord: Neither he that is sent greater than he that sent him.

John (13:16)

Jesus (Peace be upon him) saith unto her [Mary Magdalene] . . . I ascend unto my Father and your Father: And to my God, and your God.

John (20:17)

But of that day and that hour knoweth no man, not the angels which are in heaven, neither the son, but the Father.

Mark (13:32)

But now ye seek to kill me, a man that hath told you the truth, which I have heard from God.

John (8:40)

The Qur'an Speaks that Jesus (Peace be upon him) is not God

These are some extracts from the *Qur'an*, which state that Jesus (Peace be upon him) is not God.

And behold! God will say: O Jesus (Peace be upon him) son of Mary! Didst thou say unto men, worship me and my mother as gods in derogation of God?

He will say: He [Jesus] will say:

Glory to Thee!

Never could I say   ﴾وَقَالَ سُبْحَٰنَكَ مَا يَكُونُ

What I had no right (to say).   لِىٓ أَنْ أَقُولَ مَا لَيْسَ لِى

Had I said such a thing,

You would have indeed   بِحَقٍّ إِن كُنتُ قُلْتُهُ فَقَدْ

Known it.

You know what is   عَلِمْتَهُ تَعْلَمُ مَا فِى نَفْسِى

In my heart, though I

Know not what is   وَلَآ أَعْلَمُ مَا فِى نَفْسِكَ

In Thine. For You

Know in full   إِنَّكَ أَنتَ عَلَّٰمُ ٱلْغُيُوبِ ۝

All that is hidden.

Never said I to them   مَا قُلْتُ لَهُمْ إِلَّا مَآ أَمَرْتَنِى

Anything except what You:

Did command me: بِهِۦٓ أَنِ ٱعْبُدُوا۟ ٱللَّهَ رَبِّى

To say Worship

God, my Lord and your Lord . . .   وَرَبَّكُمْ﴾

Qur'an (5:116–117)

Muhammad (Peace be upon him) is not God

This verse from the *Qur'an* makes it clear that the Prophet Muhammad (Peace be upon him) is not God.

Say (O Muhammad) to the people
I am but a man like you
It is revealed to me by inspiration,
That your God is One God
So stand true to Him,
And ask for His forgiveness
And woe to those
Who join gods with God.
Qur'an (41:6)

﴿قُلْ إِنَّمَآ أَنَا۠ بَشَرٌ مِّثْلُكُمْ

يُوحَىٰٓ إِلَيَّ أَنَّمَآ إِلَٰهُكُمْ

إِلَٰهٌ وَٰحِدٌ فَٱسْتَقِيمُوٓا۟ إِلَيْهِ

وَٱسْتَغْفِرُوهُ وَوَيْلٌ

لِّلْمُشْرِكِينَ ۝﴾

Note

Some people maintain that Muslims worship Muhammad instead of God, and call themselves 'Muhammadans'. The above verse gives answer to such an allegation that Muhammad never claimed himself to be a God. He was a Prophet like any other Messenger of God. The word 'Muhammadanism' as applied to the Islamic religion is a misnomer. Islam means submission to the will of God, and its followers are called Muslims.

The authenticity of the *Qur'an*

Dr. Maurice Bucaille writes the following in his book *The Bible, the Qur'an* and *Science* on the authenticity of the *Qur'an*.

What initially strikes the reader confronted for the first time with a text (the *Qur'an*) of this kind is the sheer abundance of subjects discussed: the Creation, astronomy, the explanation of certain matters concerning the earth, the animal and vegetable kingdoms and human reproduction.

Whereas monumental errors are to be found in the Bible, I could not find a single error in the *Qur'an*. I had to stop and ask myself: if a man was the author of the *Qur'an*, how could he have written facts in the seventh century AD, that today are shown to be in keeping with modern scientific knowledge?

There was absolutely no doubt about it, the text of the *Qur'an* we have today is most definitely a text of the period, if I may be allowed to put it in these terms. What human explanation can there be for this observation? In my opinion there is no explanation; there is no special reason why an inhabitant of the Arabian Peninsula should, at a time when King Dagobert was reigning in France (ad629–639), have had scientific knowledge on certain subjects that was ten centuries ahead of our own.

Captain Jacques Cousteau, an eminent French research professor, embraced Islam as a result of reading in the *Qur'an* verses a discovery that 1,400 years ago was similar to the results of his own recent research work. The discovery is that there are phenomenal barriers at connections of certain oceans, and that the waters of one sea do not mix with that of another. The *Qur'an* clearly states the above fact.

He has let free
The two bodies
Of flowing water,
Meeting together:
Between them is a Barrier
Which they do not transgress.
Qur'an (55:19–20)

Scientific discoveries that conform with *Qur'anic* verses

Dr. Keith Moore, Professor of Anatomy (University of Toronto, Canada), describes the stages of human development in his clinically oriented book: *The Developing Human*. He discusses it in the following manner.

Growth of science was slow during the medieval period, and a few high points of embryological investigation undertaken during this age are known to us.

It is cited in the Koran *[Qur'an]*, The Holy Book of the Muslims, that human beings are produced from a mixture of secretions from the male and the female. Several references are made to the creation of a human being from a sperm drop, and it is also suggested that the resulting organism settles in the womb like a seed, six days after its beginning. The human blastocyst begins to implant about six days after fertilization. The Koran also states that the sperm drop develops 'into a congealed clot of blood.' An implanted blastocyst or a spontaneously aborted conceptus would resemble a blood clot. Reference is also made to the leech-like appearance of the embryo. The embryo shown is not unlike a leech, or a bloodsucker, in appearance.

The embryo is also said to resemble 'a chewed piece of substance' like gum or wood. The somites shown somewhat resemble the teethmarks in a chewed substance.

The developing embryo was considered to become human at forty to forty-two days and to no longer resemble an animal embryo at this stage. The human embryo begins to acquire human characteristics at this stage.

The *Qur'an* also states that the embryo develops between 'three veils of darkness.' This probably refers to (1) the maternal anterior abdominal wall, (2) the uterine wall, and (3) the amniochorionic membrane. Space does not permit discussion of several other interesting references to human prenatal development that appear in the *Qur'an*.

Sex-determining factor in the *Qur'an* and science

Many theories have been put forward to explain how the sex of a child is determined. Only recently when techniques for examining human sex cells were developed did scientists come to basically understand the sex-determining factor in human reproduction.

The human female has forty-six chromosomes in the

nucleus of each cell in the form of twenty-three matched pairs. The human male has forty-six chromosomes, but only twenty-two pairs are matched. This means that the chromosomes of one pair do not match exactly. One is the same size as those of the twenty-third pair in a female, but the other is smaller. The larger is known as the X chromosome and the smaller is the Y chromosome. Thus a woman has two X chromosomes in each cell, and a man one X and one Y chromosome.

During the reproductive process, when ovum (female sex cells) are formed, each cell contains twenty-two chromosomes and one X chromosome. However, when sperm (male sex cells) are formed, one half of the sperm will contain twenty-two chromosomes and one X chromosome, while the other half will contain twenty-two chromosomes and one Y chromosome.

During the fertilization process, if an egg is fertilized by a sperm cell bearing an X chromosome, a female offspring will result. If an egg is fertilized by a sperm bearing a Y chromosome, then the result is a sex-determining factor.

The following fourteen-hundred-year-old verses from the *Qur'an* clearly testify that the sperm cell is the sex-determining factor in human reproduction.

That He did create
In pairs, male and female;
From a seed when lodged
[In its place].
Qur'an (53:45‑46)

And God created you from dust,
Then from a sperm-drop,
Then He made you in pairs
[The male and female].
Qur'an (35:11)

مِن نُّطْفَةٍ إِذَا تُمْنَىٰ ۞﴾ ﴿وَٱللَّهُ خَلَقَكُم مِّن تُرَابٍ ثُمَّ مِن نُّطْفَةٍ ثُمَّ جَعَلَكُمْ أَزْوَٰجًا﴾

We created you from
Mixtures of germinal drop . . .
Qur'an (76:2)

﴿إِنَّا خَلَقْنَا ٱلْإِنسَٰنَ مِن نُّطْفَةٍ أَمْشَاجٍ﴾

Human development in the *Qur'an*

With regard to human development in the Qur'an Dr. Maurice Bucaille testifies that:

The *Qur'anic* description of certain stages in the development of the embryo corresponds exactly to what we today know about it, and the Qur'an does not contain a single statement that is open to criticism from modern science ... The implantation of the egg in the uterus [womb] is the result of the development of . . . formations [which] make the egg literally cling to the uterus. This is a discovery of modern times.

The act of clinging is described five different times in the *Qur'an*. Two are shown below.

Read, in the name of your Lord
And Cherisher,
Who fashioned;
Who fashioned man from
Something which clings.
Qur'an (96:1–2)

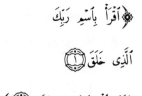

Was (man) not a small quantity
Of sperm which has been poured out?
Then did he become
Something which clings;
Then God fashioned him
In due proportion.
Qur'an (75:37–38)

The *Qur'an* informs us that the embryo subsequently passes through the stage of 'chewed flesh', then osseous tissue appears and is clad in flesh.

We fashioned ... into something
Which clings ...
Into a lump
Of flesh
In proportion and
Out of proportion ...
Qur'an (22:5)

88

We fashioned
The thing which clings
Into a chewed lump
Of flesh and
We fashioned the chewed
Flesh into bones,
And We clothed the bones
With intact flesh . . .
Qur'an (23:14)

﴾ ثُمَّ خَلَقْنَا ٱلنُّطْفَةَ عَلَقَةً فَخَلَقْنَا

ٱلْعَلَقَةَ مُضْغَةً فَخَلَقْنَا ٱلْمُضْغَةَ

عِظَٰمًا فَكَسَوْنَا ٱلْعِظَٰمَ لَحْمًا ثُمَّ

أَنشَأْنَٰهُ خَلْقًا ءَاخَرَ فَتَبَارَكَ ٱللَّهُ

أَحْسَنُ ٱلْخَٰلِقِينَ ﴿١٤﴾ ﴾

Dr. Maurice Bucaille goes on to state the following in his book.

All statements in the *Qur'an* must be compared with today's firmly established concepts. Throughout the Middle Ages, unfounded myths and speculations were at the origin of the most diversified doctrines; they persisted for several centuries after this period. It was in fact, only during the nineteenth century that people had a slightly clearer view of this question (human development).

. . . More than a thousand years before our time, at a period when whimsical doctrines still prevailed, men had a knowledge of the *Qur'an*. The statements it contains express in simple terms truths of primordial importance which man has taken centuries to discover.

Qualities for human development

The qualities for human development, according to the *Qur'an*, are: honesty, perseverance, tolerance, firmness, punctuality, courage, generosity, chastity, justice, forgiveness, and faith in the one God, Allah.

Ethics of Islam

'Imbue yourself with Divine Attributes' said the Noble Prophet (Peace be upon him).

God's attributes form the basis of Muslim ethics. Righteousness in Islam encompasses leading a life in complete harmony with the Divine attributes.

Faith and action

Faith without action is, but simply, a dead letter. Faith on its own is unstable unless translated into practice. Muslims believe that people are accountable for their own actions in this world. Each must bear his or her own burden, and nobody can expiate another's sin.

Inherent purity

Muslims believe in the inherent sinlessness of man's nature. Gifted with the power of reasoning, the human being is capable of apparently unrestricted progress. They also believe that all people are born as Muslims and that it is one's parents or guardians who initiate the deviation from or adherence to pure faith. Therefore, the term 'born Muslims' refers to those who have remained as Muslims after birth, and for those embracing Islam the term 'reverts' should be used in lieu of the misnomer 'converts'.

The position of women in Islam

Man and woman come from the same origin, possess similar souls and are gifted with equal potential for intellectual, spiritual and moral attainments. Islam places man and woman under similar obligations.

Equality of mankind and the Brotherhood of Islam

Islam is the religion of the Unity of God and the Equality of Mankind. Lineage, riches and family pride are accidental matters; virtue and the service of humanity are matters of real merit. Distinctions of colour, race and creed are non-existent within the bounds of Islam. All humans are of one family. Islam has succeeded in welding 'black' and 'white' into one fraternal whole. This strict rule of brotherhood is set firm with the following saying of the Prophet Muhammad (Peace be upon him), 'No one of you is a believer in God until he wishes for his brother what he wishes for himself'.

Personal judgement

Islam encourages the exercise of personal judgement and respects differences of opinion.

Knowledge

The pursuit of knowledge is a duty in Islam. It is the acquisition of knowledge that makes humans distinct from all other creatures.

Sanctity of Labour

Every form of labour that enables man to live honestly is respected. Idleness is reprehensible.

Charity

All the faculties of man have been given to him as a trust from God, for the benefit of his fellow creatures. It is a Muslim's duty to cater for other's needs and such charity should be applied without any discrimination. Charity in Islam brings one nearer to God, and has been made an essential part of one's obligations.

For those who give
In Charity, men and women,
And loan to God
A Beautiful Loan,
It shall be increased manifold
[To their credit], and they shall
Have [besides] a liberal reward.
Qur'an (57:18)

﴿إِنَّ ٱلْمُصَّدِّقِينَ وَٱلْمُصَّدِّقَتِ

وَأَقْرَضُوا۟ ٱللَّهَ قَرْضًا حَسَنًا

يُضَٰعَفُ لَهُمْ وَلَهُمْ أَجْرٌ

كَرِيمٌ ﴿١٨﴾﴾

Moral teachings

Islam requires the display of every quality that has been given to man, but makes only one limitation that it should be displayed on the proper occasion. It requires a person to exhibit modesty as well as boldness and courage, but at the correct moment. The *Qur'an* teaches Muslims self-respect; it allows Muslims to exercise all their rights, but not so as to violate those of others. Muslims are also required to preach the faith of Islam, but not by way of compulsion.

Those who spend [freely],
Whether in prosperity,
Or in adversity;
And pardon [all] men;

﴿ٱلَّذِينَ يُنفِقُونَ فِى ٱلسَّرَّآءِ

وَٱلضَّرَّآءِ وَٱلْكَٰظِمِينَ ٱلْغَيْظَ

For God loves those
Who do good.
Qur'an (3:134)

وَٱلۡعَافِينَ عَنِ ٱلنَّاسِۗ وَٱللَّهُ يُحِبُّ

ٱلۡمُحۡسِنِينَ ﴿١٣٤﴾

For God is with those
Who are patient,
And those who do good.
Qur'an (16:128)

﴿إِنَّ ٱللَّهَ مَعَ ٱلَّذِينَ ٱتَّقَوا۟ وَّٱلَّذِينَ

هُم مُّحۡسِنُونَ ﴿١٢٨﴾﴾

No priesthood

Islam is the way of Unity. Any association with God is direct without the mediation of a priest.

And those who,
Having done something
To be wronged their own souls,
Earnestly bring God to mind,
And ask for forgiveness
For their sins,
And who can forgive sins
Except God?
And are never obstinate
In persisting knowingly
In (the wrong) they have done
For such, the reward
Is forgiveness from their Lord ...
Qur'an (3:135–136)

﴿وَٱلَّذِينَ إِذَا فَعَلُوا۟ فَٰحِشَةً

أَوۡ ظَلَمُوٓا۟ أَنفُسَهُمۡ ذَكَرُوا۟ ٱللَّهَ

فَٱسۡتَغۡفَرُوا۟ لِذُنُوبِهِمۡ وَمَن

يَغۡفِرُ ٱلذُّنُوبَ إِلَّا ٱللَّهُ

وَلَمۡ يُصِرُّوا۟ عَلَىٰ مَا فَعَلُوا۟

وَهُمۡ يَعۡلَمُونَ ﴿١٣٥﴾ أُو۟لَٰٓئِكَ

جَزَآؤُهُم مَّغۡفِرَةٌ مِّن رَّبِّهِمۡ﴾

Forgiveness

The importance of forgiveness for a Muslim is emphasized in the following verses from the *Qur'an*.

Nor can Goodness and Evil
Be equal, Repel (evil)
With what is better:
Then will he between whom
And yourself was hatred
Become as it were
Your friend and intimate!
Qur'an (41:34)

وَلَا تَسْتَوِى ٱلْحَسَنَةُ وَلَا
ٱلسَّيِّئَةُ ٱدْفَعْ بِٱلَّتِى هِىَ أَحْسَنُ
فَإِذَا ٱلَّذِى بَيْنَكَ وَبَيْنَهُ عَدَاوَةٌ
كَأَنَّهُ وَلِىٌّ حَمِيمٌ ۝

Tell those who believe,
To forgive those who
Do not look forward
To the Days of God.
Qur'an (45:14)

قُل لِّلَّذِينَ ءَامَنُوا يَغْفِرُوا
لِلَّذِينَ لَا يَرْجُونَ أَيَّامَ ٱللَّهِ

Kind words
And the covering of faults (of others)
Are better than charity
Followed by injury.
Allah is Free of all wants,
And He is Most Forbearing.
Qur'an (2:263)

قَوْلٌ مَّعْرُوفٌ وَمَغْفِرَةٌ
خَيْرٌ مِّن صَدَقَةٍ يَتْبَعُهَآ
أَذًى وَٱللَّهُ غَنِىٌّ
حَلِيمٌ ۝

Part III

Other Important Questions

How do Muslims treat the elderly?

In the Islamic world there are no old people's homes. The strain of caring for one's parents in the most difficult time of their lives is considered to be an honour and blessing, and an opportunity for great spiritual growth. God asks that we not only pray for our parents, but also act with limitless compassion, remembering that when we were helpless children they preferred us to themselves. Mothers are particularly honoured.

The Prophet (Peace be upon him) taught that 'Paradise lies at the feet of mothers'. When they reach old age, Muslim parents are treated mercifully, with the same kindness and selflessness.

In Islam, serving one's parents is a duty second only to prayer, and it is their right to expect it. It is considered to be despicable to express any irritation when, through no fault of their own, the old become difficult (*Qur'an* 17:23–4).

How do Muslims view death?

Like Jews and Christians, Muslims believe that the present life is only a preparation for the next realm of existence.

Basic articles of faith include: Resurrection, the Day of Judgement, Heaven and Hell. When a Muslim dies, he or she is washed, usually by a family member, wrapped in a clean white cloth and buried preferably on the same day. A simple prayer follows. Muslims consider this one of the final services they can do for their relatives and an opportunity to remember their own brief existence here on earth. The Prophet (Peace be upon him) taught that three things can continue to help a person even after death: charity that he had given, knowledge that he had taught and prayers on their behalf by a righteous offspring.

What does Islam say about war?

Like Christianity, Islam permits fighting in self-defence, in defence of religion, or on the behalf of those who have been expelled forcibly from their homes. It lays down strict rules of combat, which include prohibitions against harming civilians and against destroying crops, trees and livestock. As Muslims see it, injustice would be triumphant in the world if good men were not prepared to risk their lives for a righteous cause. The Qur'an says:

Fight in the cause of God against those who fight you, but do not transgress limits. God does not love transgressors.

Qur'an (2:190)

If they seek peace, then you should also seek peace. And trust in Allah for He is the One that hears and knows all things.

Qur'an (8:61)

War, therefore, is the last resort, and is subject to the rigorous conditions laid down by the sacred law. The term *jihad* literally means 'struggle', and Muslims believe that there are two kinds of *jihad*: the outer struggle against the forces of evil and corruption, and the inner 'struggle' that everyone wages against egotistic desires, for the sake of attaining inner peace.

How does Islam guarantee human rights?

Freedom of conscience is laid down by the *Qur'an* itself: 'There is no compulsion in religion' (*Qur'an* 2:256).

The life and property of all citizens in an Islamic state are considered to be sacred whether a person is Muslim or not.

Racism is incomprehensible to Muslims, for the *Qur'an* speaks of human equality in the following terms.

O mankind! We created you from a single soul, male and female, and made you into nations and tribes, so that you may come to know one another. Truly, the most honored of you in Allah's sight is the greatest of you in piety. Allah is All-Knowing, All-Aware.

Qur'an (49:13)

The Muslim World

The Muslim population of the world is around one billion. Most Muslims live east of Karachi. Thirty per cent of Muslims live in the Indian subcontinent, 20 per cent in Sub-Saharan Africa, 17 per cent in Southeast Asia, 18 per cent in the Arab world, 10 per cent in the Soviet Union and China. Turkey, Iran and Afghanistan comprise 10 per cent of the non-Arab Middle East. Although there are Muslim minorities in almost every region, including Latin America and Australia, they are most numerous in the Soviet Union, India, China and Central Africa. There are five million Muslims in the United States.

Islam in the United States

It is almost impossible to generalize about American Muslims: converts, immigrants, factory workers and doctors, all are making their own contribution to America's future. This complex community is unified by a common faith, underpinned by a countrywide network of more than a thousand mosques.

Muslims were early arrivals in North America. By the eighteenth century there were many thousands of them, working as slaves on plantations. These early communities, cut off from their heritage and families, inevitably lost their Islamic identity as time went by. Today many Afro-American Muslims play an important role in the Islamic community.

The nineteenth century, however, saw the beginnings of an influx of Arab Muslims, most of whom settled in the major industrial centres where they worshipped in hired rooms. The early twentieth century witnessed the arrival of several hundred thousand Muslims from Eastern Europe: the first Albanian mosque was opened in Maine in 1915; others soon followed, and a group of Polish Muslims opened a mosque in Brooklyn in 1928.

In 1947, the Washington Islamic Center was founded during the term of President Truman, and several nationwide organizations were set up in the 1950s. During the 50s and through the 70s there was a great influx of Muslims from India and Pakistan who today represent a major segment of immigrant American Muslims. From the early 20s until the 70s, a few pseudo-Islamic organizations appeared among indigenous Muslims using Islamic terminology to cover racist un-Islamic teachings: the Nation of Islam (commonly called 'Black Muslims'), the Moorish Science Temple, the Ansarullah and others. Although they have always remained a small but vocal minority, some of their spokesmen continue to tarnish the image of Islam until today. The Muslim population in America today is estimated by researchers to be between five and eight million.

O mankind! We created you from a single soul, male and female, and made you into nations and tribes, so that you may come to know one another. Truly, the most honoured of you in Allah's sight is the greatest of you in piety. Allah is All-knowing, All-aware.

Qur'an (49:13)

﴿يَٰٓأَيُّهَا ٱلنَّاسُ إِنَّا خَلَقْنَٰكُم مِّن ذَكَرٍ وَأُنثَىٰ وَجَعَلْنَٰكُمْ شُعُوبًا وَقَبَآئِلَ لِتَعَارَفُوٓا۟

إِنَّ أَكْرَمَكُمْ عِندَ ٱللَّهِ أَتْقَىٰكُمْ إِنَّ ٱللَّهَ عَلِيمٌ خَبِيرٌ ۝﴾